POLITICS FOR
SOCIAL WORKERS

POLITICS FOR SOCIAL WORKERS

A Practical Guide to Effecting Change

STEPHEN PIMPARE

Columbia University Press

New York

Columbia University Press
Publishers Since 1893
New York   Chichester, West Sussex
cup.columbia.edu

Library of Congress Cataloging-in-Publication Data
Names: Pimpare, Stephen, author.
Title: Politics for social workers : a practical guide to effecting
change / Stephen Pimpare.
Description: New York City : Columbia University Press, 2021.
| Includes index.
Identifiers: LCCN 2021022070 (print) | LCCN 2021022071 (ebook)
| ISBN 9780231196925 (hardback) | ISBN 9780231196932 (trade
paperback) | ISBN 9780231551892 (ebook)
Subjects: LCSH: Social service—Political aspects. | Social workers.
Classification: LCC HV40 .P546 2021 (print) |
LCC HV40 (ebook) | DDC 361.3—dc23
LC record available at https://lccn.loc.gov/2021022070
LC ebook record available at https://lccn.loc.gov/2021022071

Cover design: Elliott S. Cairns

CONTENTS

CONTENTS

PREFACE

POLICY HISTORIANS write about the two "big bangs" of U.S. welfare state development—the New Deal programs of the 1930s and the Great Society programs of the 1960s. You might encounter others describing these moments as "critical junctures."

Could March 2020 and the onset of the COVID-19 pandemic have marked the beginning of a third big bang? Did we enter another critical juncture in our political and policy history?

In that month alone, so much of what for years we had been told could not be done was done almost overnight. Congress enacted a national paid sick leave policy (albeit a temporary one), ending our status as the only rich democracy without one. It instituted a national emergency unemployment insurance program to supplement the state-run plans, and a relatively generous one at that, sending an additional $600 per week to people who could not work (and expanding the definition of who was eligible), then extending it at $300 per week at the end of the year. It suspended student loan payments for six months (and later extended that for an even longer period) and authorized the federal government to send a cash payment of up to $1,200 per adult and $500 per child to almost every family in the country (subsequently doing it again at half the amount). These initiatives were bold enough that household income actually rose and poverty rates declined (J. Han, Meyer, and Sullivan 2020; Parolin, Curran, and Wimer 2020; DeParle 2020) even though the most comprehensive official unemployment measure exceeded 20 percent at one point that year (U.S. Bureau of Labor Statistics 2020). And even if it was short-lived, many of Washington's reliable deficit hawks (people who worry a lot about the size of federal deficits, or pretend that they do) recognized the urgent need for action and debt-financed spending.

Meanwhile, states eased eligibility for their own unemployment programs, suspended work requirements for Medicaid and the Supplemental Nutrition Assistance Program (SNAP, what we used to call Food Stamps), expanded SNAP eligibility and increased benefit levels, created emergency funds to support day-care facilities, opened up new shelter spaces for people who were experiencing homelessness, and released people who had been incarcerated for trivial offenses or who had served a significant percentage of their sentence. Nonviolent offenders were issued warnings instead of being arrested. Governments encouraged (or required) localities to suspend evictions and eliminate penalties for late property-tax payments, directed public utilities not to cut off water or power for people who fell behind on their bills, and advised local authorities to equip the camps set up by homeless people with portable bathrooms and washing stations. Many cities reconfigured their public spaces, closing more of them to cars and making them available to pedestrians, cyclists, diners, and children at play.

Businesses raised workers' wages (although making sure to note that such increases were temporary), and people started to earnestly thank grocery store clerks, delivery people, and health-care workers for their service just as they had previously done for veterans of the U.S. armed forces. In some places, homeless people claimed and occupied vacant, abandoned properties that were owned by the city. A smattering of strikes by frontline service and delivery workers spread throughout the country, causing still more businesses to raise wages, provide protective equipment, and promise safer working conditions. And in what may be one of the greatest acts of mass solidarity of the era, untold millions of us remained sequestered in our homes in order to stop the spread of the disease and protect our neighbors from illness or death.

To be sure, even this crisis was not enough to get Congress to enact the more radical proposals that were before it in those early months—a permanent national unemployment insurance program guaranteeing that people receive 100 percent of their former wages, abolition of student loan debt, a nationwide rent and mortgage moratorium, expanded access to Medicaid and Medicare, or stricter occupational health and safety regulations for the most at-risk occupations. Farmworkers and meat-processing-plant employees, many of whom were undocumented, continued to feed the nation while being ineligible for any of the expanded relief programs. Immigration and Customs

Enforcement (ICE) continued to capture and imprison immigrants and refugees (kidnapping and then losing track of their children in the process), and, even with state, county, and municipal action, by midyear the COVID-19 death rate for prisoners was 5.5 times higher than the overall rate (Saloner et al. 2020). By May 2020 that sense of urgency and solidarity seemed to have left Washington, D.C., even though more than 100,000 people had already been officially counted among the dead at that point.

Then, yet another Black man was killed by the police—this time, his name was George Floyd—and a massive wave of sustained protest swept through the nation, inspiring comparisons to the "unrest" of the 1960s and generating concern that the United States was slipping into irredeemable chaos. As has historically been the case, much of the violence that occurred was instigated by agents of the state, not those protesting the aggressively racist practices of its institutions (Chenoweth and Pressman 2020). In response to those events, states and localities started what in some cases were serious conversations about reducing the portion of their budgets allocated to police forces ("Defund the Police" became a rallying cry). Citizens toppled statues and defaced monuments erected to the Confederacy, and many finally came to recognize the Confederate battle flag as an inherently racist symbol; NASCAR and the U.S. Navy even banned its display. These were the largest sustained mass protests the United States had seen since the peak of the Black rights movements of the 1960s and perhaps the largest in our history (International Council for Diplomacy and Dialogue 2020; Putnam, Chenoweth, and Pressman 2020)—another extraordinary instance of mass solidarity.

As is common during crises (N. Klein 2007), bad actors will seize such moments to enact their preferred policy changes. The Trump administration used the pandemic, economic uncertainty, and outrage over racist state violence as cover for rolling back environmental protections; accelerating anti-immigrant policies and border closures; firing oversight officials perceived as hostile to their autocratic impulses or impeding their efforts to profit from the crisis; continuing efforts to corrupt the decennial census count; delegitimizing absentee-voting methods and undermining the 2020 election; and engaging in increasingly aggressive extraconstitutional efforts to suppress speech and assault protesters, culminating in the deployment of armed federal troops to stir unrest in Democratic-leaning cities and voicing support for right-wing terrorists who murdered protesters. Many worried about rising authoritarianism and "democratic backsliding" (Ingraham 2020a; Bright Line Watch 2020), concerns that gained added weight as defeated president Donald Trump waged a sustained coup effort after losing to incoming president Joe Biden (Rutenberg and Corasaniti 2020). Although the presidential transition ratcheted down the immediate threat, the risk remains.

What does this all tell us about U.S. politics and policy making? Do these extraordinary events confirm what we thought we knew about politics and power in the United States, or do they require us to rethink our assumptions? And, most important, what lessons can you, as social workers and others working with and for marginalized populations, take away from this extended series of crises that will help you advocate for and enact policies to improve the well-being of the people and places you care about? What are the strategic lessons from 2020 that will help you fight successfully for change into the future? It is my hope that this book will help you begin to answer those questions for yourself and to think strategically about what you can do to effect change.

POLITICS FOR
SOCIAL WORKERS

INTRODUCTION

MUCH OF the thinking about and writing of this book predates the extraordinary events of 2020, but its goals remain the same.

First, it aims to help you develop a better understanding of U.S. political systems and the operations of our politics and policy making, which can be confounding. Because we have such a complicated political setup, it's hard to know who has the power to make change. It's doubly hard to spur action on behalf of marginalized populations and hard to know where to place blame when we don't. These challenges are even more acute in our era of hyperpolarized politics.

This book offers social work students, instructors, and practitioners a new resource to deepen their policy knowledge by bringing research from political science, policy studies, and American political development to bear. Here you will find a more critical and informed view of what political scientists (think they) know about how politics really works, where power really resides, how both big and incremental changes occur, how policy programs are structured, and how policy affects general attitudes about government and even a client's willingness to participate in a range of civic activities. It also engages in some myth busting, emphasizing the limits of what can be achieved through dialogue and debate with those who disagree with us, the reasons advocates for marginalized populations can sometimes be so ineffective in national politics, and how what appear to be bugs in the political system are, in fact, features.

Second, this book will help you to develop sustainable strategies to act on that knowledge at the micro, meso, and macro levels. Each chapter, some of which are quite brief, concludes with a "Lessons for Practice" section, applying what you have just read to practical aspects of your life as a citizen and as a professional.

As you likely know, accreditation standards for schools of social work require that students not only understand the federal and state social welfare policies that affect their clients, but also engage in "policy practice." The National Association of Social Workers (NASW) Code of Ethics similarly obligates practitioners to "engage in social and political action," "advocate for changes in policy" that benefit vulnerable populations, and "promote social justice" (National Association of Social Workers 2017; Council on Social Work Education 2015). But how can you, busy with a full caseload, make time for activism? What should the average social worker who has one free afternoon per week focus on? Where does one begin?

This book is something to add to your tool kit as you think about how you want to fulfill those obligations and what you can do to help build a more inclusive and responsive politics. It does this through practical, hands-on steps that readers can take to effect change in their agencies, their neighborhoods, their towns and cities, their states, and Washington, DC. It takes seriously that complexity, foregrounding the ways in which good strategy and successful interventions will vary from policy issue to policy issue, from place to place, and from time to time—there is no one universal strategy for enacting change, just as there is no simple, universal clinical intervention to be applied to all clients, even if their problems might, at first, present similarly. Every political and policy challenge is distinct, just as every person, family, or community has its own strengths and its own obstacles to overcome.

Altering power relations in an unequal and undemocratic polity is not easy. But our response to the daunting challenges we and our clients face cannot be cynicism, apathy, or despair. Instead, we need to develop the knowledge and acquire the skills to design and carry out strategically sound plans for change in a system that will resist those efforts at every turn. Social work education needs a theory of power and political action rooted in a hardheaded, clear-eyed worldview, and *Politics for Social Workers* seeks to do just that by bringing in research and perspectives from the disciplines that focus most intensely on these questions.

This is not meant to suggest that social work is inferior to political science or to castigate social workers for not knowing more about the research in other disciplines—indeed, I'd venture to say that social workers probably know more about political science and policy research than political scientists know about social work research. Rather, it is to argue, from the perspective of a person who has had their feet in both worlds, that there are some particular insights from political science that will make social work better, smarter, and more effective. It is not the task of this book, but political science could learn from social work, too. While it has made progress in this regard, political science still overprivileges quantitative methods and remains too reluctant to weigh in on current political issues. As political scientist Rogers Smith (2015, 367) put it, "the discipline has over time given greater priority to becoming more truly scientific, rather than to contributing to democracy or America—while continuing to seek to minimize the tensions among those goals. That trend has persisted despite periodic outbursts of resistance."

Social work, to its credit, has had no such reluctance to engage in urgent issues of the day. But it can be naïve about obstacles to change and blind to the reasons that poor and marginalized populations are poor and marginalized to begin with. I've often heard social work students in policy classes, when asked to propose solutions to particularly thorny problems, suggest that what we need to do is to better inform the public, to educate, and to let people know just how bad things are. What happens next is often left unspoken, as is how that knowledge gets turned into policy change. There's often a black-box problem here—or what a *South Park* viewer might recognize as Underpants Gnomes logic (Parker 1998):

Step 1: Educate people
Step 2: ?
Step 3: Social justice

This is a trap that even experienced practitioners and senior academics fall into, evidenced by the frequency with which social work journals publish articles that are "calls to action." Examples are easy to find in even a cursory search of recent papers: "Calling Social Work to the Movement for Educational Justice" (Ball 2020); "A Call to Action for Social Work: Minimizing Financial Hardship for Families of Children with Special Health Care Needs" (Bachman and Comeau 2010); "School Social Workers: A Call to Action in Support of Human Rights" (Villarreal Sosa and Nuckolls 2018); "A Call to Action: Domestic Violence Education in Social Work" (Crabtree-Nelson, Grossman, and Lundy 2016); "Men's Mental Health: A Call to Social Workers" (Shafer and Wendt 2015); "Social Justice and Civil Rights: A Call to Action for Social Work" (Bent-Goodley and Hopps 2017); "Civilian Social Work with Veterans Returning from Iraq and Afghanistan: A Call to Action" (Rubin 2012); "At the Intersection of COVID-19 and Sex Work in the United States: A Call for Social Work Action" (Bromfield, Panichelli, and Capous-Desyllas 2021). To implore people to pay more attention to one particular issue is not the same as outlining a practicable agenda for making things better.

What if the problem is not that people (and people holding political office) don't know just how cruel, irrational, inefficient, or discriminatory policies are or how ignored are some populations in need, but that they simply don't care? Or, to put it more charitably, that they care about other things more? This is an agenda-setting problem, to be sure, but it is more than that. It is a problem not of persuasion but of *power*. The task in that instance is either to find a way to force people to do something they do not want to do or to replace them with people who already share your goals.

I hope this book will help you develop a deeper, more sophisticated analysis and a sound action plan for advancing the issues you care about. Two things give me confidence that this kind of reallocation of power and positive change is possible: the experience of almost every other rich democracy on the planet, each of which has devised ways to better serve its population and improve well-being than the United States has, and our own history, which provides some very particular lessons to be drawn from the Reconstruction, Great Depression, and post–World War II periods.

This is a dark time in the life of the United States. The populations we serve are under assault and at risk. But it's always an urgent time for social work and social workers, and it is always a dark time for someone. In these pages, I strive to offer a guide that will be applicable to any moment in political time, whether we judge it to be one that is particularly friendly to reformist interventions and improving the well-being of marginalized populations or one that seems especially hostile to the ideals and values embedded in the NASW Code of Ethics.

Let's start with some myth busting. . . .

Chapter One

THE U.S. CONSTITUTION
IS UNDEMOCRATIC

IT HAS been common in political science to describe the U.S. political system as a generally open, pluralist one, in which a group's influence is roughly equal to its numbers and the intensity of its activism. This is the expectation about how the Constitution would work that is offered throughout *The Federalist Papers*, the editorials that Alexander Hamilton, James Madison, and John Jay ([1788] 1992) wrote to persuade people to support their proposed new government, and it's an idea that since then has been at the heart of both scholarship on U.S. democracy and popular conceptions of it (Smith 1993). However imperfectly, this thinking goes, the U.S. system seeks to identify the desires of the majority and then works to translate them into particular action. It is *democratic*.

There have been notable challenges to this view from a number of scholars, including C. Wright Mills ([1956] 2000), G. William Domhoff (2007, 2014), and Frances Fox Piven and

Richard A. Cloward (1993). E. E. Schattschneider may have offered the most succinct and enduring assessment: "The flaw in the Pluralist heaven," he wrote in 1960, "is that the heavenly chorus sings with a strong upper-class accent. Probably about 90 percent of the people cannot get into the pressure system" (Schattschneider [1960] 1975, 34–35). But those critiques were the exceptions rather than the rule, and in the past they were not treated seriously by the discipline (Block and Piven 2010).

The consensus has finally started to catch up, however. Surely part of the explanation is that economic inequality in the United States has reached record levels, exceeding even that of the Gilded Age or the 1920s, and more people have become aware of this and supportive of policies that would restore some balance (Page and Jacobs 2009). A host of "mainstream" political scientists have added empirical meat to those once radical claims, helping to fuel more recent complaints from Occupy Wall Street and other movement actors that our system is dominated by elites (Bartels 2016; Gilens 2012; Gilens and Page 2014; Hacker and Pierson 2010; Page and Gilens 2017; Schakel, Burgoon, and Hakhverdian 2020), complaints that are bolstered by increasingly fine-grained evidence of income and wealth inequality produced by historically minded economists (Piketty and Goldhammer 2017; Saez and Zucman 2016, 2019, 2020).

So it is no longer unusual for political scientists employed by elite institutions to publish articles in top-tier journals in which they try to explain how it is that such high and still growing rates of wealth and income inequality can persist in a supposedly democratic polity. Adam Bonica and his colleagues offered five possible explanations for how this happens: credulous acceptance of neoliberal ideology and trickle-down economic theories; low voting rates among poor and low-income populations, which reduces their influence; rising overall levels of income and wealth, which tamp down dissatisfaction among those who benefit; the disproportionate influence of wealthy individuals in our political systems; and the potentially undemocratic features of our core political institutions (Bonica et al. 2013). As noted above, it has long seemed obvious to some that economic inequality is an essential fact of life here, that it was both cause and consequence of our distorted allocations of political power, and that we therefore need to pay attention to politics as much as economics in order to explain it. But that this is now a relatively mundane position is perhaps indicative of just how bad things have gotten: even elite academics can see it.

One of the most direct assaults on the idea that we inhabit an open, democratic system was a 2014 article that sought to test core theories of power and politics in the United States. What the authors found, as Mills, Domhoff, Piven and Cloward, and others had been trying to tell us for many decades, is that we do not in fact have a pluralist system but one that has always been skewed to the advantage of wealthier, white interests (and, more recently, one whose proclivity toward authoritarianism and oligarchy has become harder to ignore). As they summarize, "The central point that emerges from our research is that economic elites and organized groups representing business interests have substantial independent impacts on U.S. government policy, while mass-based interest groups and average citizens have little or no independent influence" (Gilens and Page 2014, 565). This confirms what Martin Gilens has reported elsewhere (Gilens

2012): The more that economic elites support a particular policy change, the more likely it is to be enacted into law, but when low- or middle-income people favor a particular change, it has no measurable effect on the likelihood it will be adopted. They refer to this as a system of economic-elite domination.

A turning point in the acceptance of these once derided viewpoints might have been when Robert Dahl, an eminent scholar of the discipline whose early work sits at the very heart of the pluralist view of political power, published an extended catalogue of the U.S. Constitution's undemocratic features (Dahl 2003, 2005). Those qualities of the Constitution include the fact that it didn't merely protect our especially brutal form of chattel slavery but actually rewarded slaveholding states thanks to the "three-fifths clause" (Article I, Section 2), which counted enslaved people as three-fifths of a person for purposes of allocating representation in the House of Representatives. The more enslaved people there were in your state, the more House members you were entitled to (but those enslaved people could not vote, of course). And the only office in the new Constitution that was directly elected were members of the House of Representatives; senators were elected by state legislatures until the Seventeenth Amendment was ratified in 1913. One way to think of the U.S. Constitution is that it granted what at the time really were unusually expansive rights to "ordinary" citizens (even if that then meant only white men who owned property) and designed the rest of the system to limit the ability of that mass democratic power to act too easily. What you may remember as "separated powers" and "checks and balances" reflect a government of "separated institutions *sharing* powers"

(Neustadt 1991, 29), in which all must cooperate for anything to get done.

The U.S. Constitution thereby sets up a government that is at war with itself. One of the problems its architects were trying to solve was how to ensure that too much power was not concentrated in a single office or person, having learned the dangers of that from their experience with King George III. If you read the *Federalist Papers*, you can see a fairly cynical reading of human nature underlying their thinking; much of the Rube Goldberg–style contraption they designed was an effort to construct a system that, on the one hand, accounted for the fact that "enlightened statesmen will not always be at the helm" and, on the other, reflected a fear that too much democratic control in the hands of the majority could put minorities at risk. There has been much debate over which minorities they were most concerned with protecting; one famous account (Beard 1914) makes the case that it was themselves—property-owning white men, many of whom were enslavers—about whom they were most worried. Beard is often criticized for offering too crude an analysis, but there is now a long line of research buttressing the case that the U.S. system is especially favorable to the concerns of the rich and to organized business interests (Lindblom 1982, 1995), groups still overrepresented in Congress, as we'll see in chapters to come.

The Senate still provides people throughout the country with dramatically unequal representation: each state, no matter how large or how small, gets the same number of votes (two). It's the same for California, with a 2019 population of 39.5 million, as it is for Wyoming, with a population of under 579,000. Residents of Puerto Rico and the District of Columbia—some 1.5 percent of the U.S. population—have no voting congressional representatives at all (USDA Economic Research Service 2020). If current population and residency trends continue, by 2040, 70 percent of the population will collectively be represented by only thirty-two of the one hundred senators (Bump 2018). It's not merely that this gives disproportionate power to smaller states; because of how people are distributed, it gives disproportionate power to less-educated whites in particular (McAuliffe 2019). We can see this in the composition of the Senate that was seated in 2021, in which whites, gun owners, and rural areas were overrepresented while Black populations were underrepresented and Asian and Latino populations were wildly underrepresented (Ettlinger and Hensley 2020).

Because our method of electing the president, the Electoral College, awards votes based on each state's combined House and Senate membership, this imbalance is reinscribed there; this can create some perverse results, in which a candidate can win many more total votes and yet still get fewer votes in the Electoral College. This is how we got Donald Trump as president, even though his opponent, Hillary Clinton, had some three million more ballots cast on her behalf; it's even odder than that, given that if we could disperse just 77,000 or so votes from her four-million-vote margin of victory in California across Pennsylvania, Wisconsin, and Michigan, she would have won the Electoral College too—without changing the overall vote totals. This undemocratic outcome has happened before: in 1824, 1876, 1888, and 2000, the candidate who earned fewer votes nonetheless became president.

After the 2020 results were in, Democrats had won the popular vote—they received more overall votes than Republicans—in seven of the eight previous presidential elections (B. Clinton, B. Clinton, Gore, Obama, Obama, H. R. Clinton, Biden) yet only assumed the presidency five times (B. Clinton twice, Obama twice, then Biden). Yes, this is the way the Electoral College works, but this is not how elections function anywhere else in the world or even in any other U.S. state or local election. The common arguments in favor of it—that it ensures that candidates campaign in all parts of the country, protects the interests of less populous states, simplifies electoral processes in a large republic, or helps maintain federalism—do not bear up under scrutiny (Wegman 2020).

Our system also grants unusually broad powers to the federal courts, and to the Supreme Court in particular, which has taken for itself the ability to overturn democratically enacted decisions of legislatures (Ferejohn 2002; *Marbury v. Madison* 1803); this is antimajoritarian, creating opportunities for policy making by the courts if efforts fail in the lawmaking process. Federal judges are nominated by the president, who is elected through an undemocratic system, and confirmed by the Senate, which is also undemocratic in the ways we have seen. One of the consequences is that five of the six conservative justices on the Supreme Court as of this writing (Roberts, Alito, Gorsuch, Kavanaugh, Barrett)—who may be setting national policy for a generation or more—were appointed by presidents who did not initially ascend to office with the support of a majority (or even a plurality) of voters. Further, because the built-in bias of the Senate gives disproportionate power to less populated states, the last three were confirmed even though senators representing a majority of the U.S. population voted *against* their confirmation (GovTrack 2018; Millhiser 2020).

Finally, the filibuster rule of the Senate, which requires that there be sixty "yes" votes to proceed on certain categories of legislation, is yet another opportunity for a minority of senators to override the wishes of a majority.

This is rule by the minority (and a white minority at that)—a principle that, as far as I can tell, is nowhere held up as a sound principle of democratic governance. We are so used to these anomalies that we fail to appreciate how irrational and unjust they are.

LESSONS FOR PRACTICE

I wrote above about how long it took for "mainstream" political scientists to recognize what "radicals" had been saying for decades. There's an important lesson here: Radical analyses and proposals are only radical until they are not. Think of any advance in social, political, or economic equality that we today generally accept as obviously right and just—women voting, the formal illegality of race-based discrimination, laws against child labor, civil marriage for same-sex couples, rights afforded to transgender people—these were all ridiculously radical notions once. Do not be cowed if people tell you that your goal is impractical, overambitious, unrealistic, or destabilizing. Do keep in mind the lessons from throughout this book about the challenges of policy making in complex, layered, path-dependent systems, but hold firm to the historical lesson that what's radical today is commonplace tomorrow, and we only get to tomorrow thanks to the hard work of the radicals today.

There's another thing to keep in mind: While in the U.S. system elites may win a lot, they do not always win. As the sociologist Fred Block put it long ago, "The ruling class does not rule" (Block 1977). Or as another scholar observed more recently, "Political control is always partial and incomplete" (Sheingate 2014, 464). There is always a space to contest current politics and policy, if you are diligent about seeking it out.

Chapter Two

OUR REPRESENTATIVE INSTITUTIONS
ARE NOT REPRESENTATIVE

IT IS not just that the institutions of U.S. policy making are skewed in favor of minority interests; the elected officials who occupy those institutions are unrepresentative of the population at large. That's true even though the 116th Congress (2019–2020) was at that time the most racially diverse in our history, with just over 10 percent of the House and Senate identifying as Black (compared to about 13 percent in the population overall), just under 10 percent Hispanic or Latino (compared to 18 percent), almost 4 percent Asian, Pacific Islander, or South Asian (versus 6 percent overall), and a total of four Native Americans (less than 1 percent, vs. 1.3 percent overall). A total of 13 percent were immigrants or the children of immigrants (versus 28 percent of the population). There was also a record number of women, 24 percent of the House and Senate combined, although more than half the total U.S. population are women; this record high still places us among the OECD countries with the smallest share of women in the national legislature. More than one-third of congressional Democrats, but less than 10 percent of Republicans, were women (Congressional Research Service 2020; Geiger 2019; World Bank 2019). The 117th Congress saw an even larger share of women and women of color (Center for American Women and Politics 2020), along with a record number of lesbian, gay and bisexual members (Flores et al. 2020). Progress is good, and it is important to celebrate it, but we still have work to do if we think that this kind of representation matters—and the research tells us that it does (Espírito-Santo, Freire, and Serra-Silva 2020; N. E. Brown and Gershon 2016; M. C. Matthews 2019; Reingold, Haynie, and Widner 2021).

Just as important for our purposes, and a dimension along which there is no progress to celebrate, is the unrepresentativeness of members in terms of income and wealth. In that same 116th Congress, the median net worth was $1 million, meaning that half of all members had that much wealth or more (with the richest senator worth $260 million and the richest House member $189 million). By contrast, median household income in the country as a whole was just under $62,000 in 2018 ($41,511 for Black households), and median net worth (for 2016) was $101,800; the median wealth of Black households in that year was $17,150 (but $171,000 for white families) (Evers-Hilstrom 2020; Guzman 2019; Horowitz, Igielnik, and Kochhar 2020; McIntosh et al. 2020).

These developments coincide with a decline in the number of people in Congress who come from working-class backgrounds (that number was never very high, though higher historically in state legislatures than in Congress), and there is evidence that if Congress better reflected the national at large it would vote differently (Carnes 2012, 2013, 2018; Griffin and Anewalt-Remsburg 2013; Kraus and Callaghan 2014).

Perhaps as a consequence of their wealth and class status, members of Congress overestimate the conservatism of their constituents, and they vote accordingly. Elected officials may genuinely think that their votes represent the wishes of their districts, but they are off by twenty percentage points on gun control and almost ten percentage points on abortion policy, for example. This effect is larger and more common among Republicans, but Democrats also overestimate the conservatism of their constituents—in part because conservative constituents are more likely to reach out to their elected representatives (Broockman and Skovron 2018). This could also be a consequence of "exclusion bias." That is, people who have direct experience of welfare-state programs and others who support them may be less inclined to respond to questions about that experience in opinion surveys than those with more conservative, antiwelfare opinions, thereby producing biased results (Berinsky 2002); people experiencing homelessness and people without access to phones, moreover, are totally excluded from telephone surveys.

This is consistent with one of Suzanne Mettler's findings. As she summarizes: "those whose voices are heard most loudly by policy-makers use plenty of social policies themselves, but they are typically policies that obscure government's role, whereas those who use more visible policies, particularly means-tested ones, are more aware of government's role, but they are less likely to be active in politics. This participatory tilt means that policy-makers receive less support for strengthening and expanding social provisions than they would if citizens spoke in politics with equal voices" (Mettler 2019). (See chapter 12 for more on these "hidden" welfare-state programs.)

LESSONS FOR PRACTICE

While we still have much distance to travel before we achieve proportionate representation for each of the many diverse groups that make up our nation, notice how much more diverse the Democratic coalition is than the Republican one. If you find yourself complaining that the Democrats do not effectively represent you and your clients as aggressively or as often as you wish, part of the explanation is that the task of building legislative majorities is harder for the Democrats precisely because of that diversity. They have more divergent interests to try to satisfy, so part of your challenge will be to get more members of that unwieldy coalition to support your issues.

If even Democratic elected officials enact policies that are more conservative than their constituents would prefer because they are more likely to be contacted by their more conservative citizens, that's easy to fix—call, write, and show up at town hall meetings to voice your opinions, and get your colleagues, clients, friends, and family to do the same (for some tips on effective communication strategies, see this book's conclusion). Some research shows that when politicians are better informed about overall public opinion in their districts their votes better represent those residents (Butler and Nickerson 2011). So if there are reputable polls that support your case, make sure your elected officials know about them; if there are no polling data available, see if a local university is willing conduct a poll on the subject or ask a local news outlet to add a question about your issue to its next poll. As I will emphasize throughout this book, there are lots of opportunities for you to build networks of influence and to have an impact at the local level—when in doubt, start there.

Chapter Three

WE'RE TERRIBLE AT
CONDUCTING ELECTIONS

THESE UNDEMOCRATIC features of the U.S. constitutional system endure in part because we have rather anemic participation rates and because we do not consistently run free and fair elections—all of this despite our propensity to boast to the world of our status as a model democracy.

Voting rates are typically lower in the United States than they are in many other democracies. More than 80 percent of the voting-age population in Belgium, Sweden, and Denmark votes; the figure is 70 percent or more in eight additional wealthy nations, and regularly more than 60 percent in eleven others (DeSilver 2018b). By contrast, turnout in most recent U.S. presidential elections has been under 60 percent of eligible voters (it was 56 percent in 2016) and even lower in "off-year" or midterm elections, when there is no presidential campaign but all members of the House and about one third of senators are up for election. However, with an overall turnout rate of

53.4 percent, the 2018 midterm had the highest rate in forty years, thanks in part to a large increase in younger voters, and the 2020 presidential election saw a turnout of 66.7 percent, the highest since 1900 (File 2017; Misra 2019; DeSilver 2018b; McDonald 2020). Participation is even lower for state and local elections (for representatives in your state legislature and for governor, mayor, city counselor, alder board, school board, district attorney, local judges, and so on), when turnout rates can be in the single digits (Portland State University and the Knight Foundation 2016).

Some groups are more likely to vote than others. As a rule, lower-income, less-educated people of color are least likely to vote; those who are white, over age sixty-five, and with advanced degrees tend to be the most reliable participants. Among people who do vote, there are partisan patterns. In 2016, majorities of women (about 54 percent, depending on the data source), college-degree holders (57 percent), African Americans (91 percent), Hispanic Americans (66 percent), Asian Americans (65 percent), Jews (71 percent), LGBT populations (78 percent), atheists or agnostics (69 percent), and people under the age of thirty (58 percent) voted for the Democratic presidential candidate, Hillary Clinton. The core Republican constituencies were men (52 percent voted for Donald Trump), people over age sixty-five (53 percent), whites (54 percent), whites without a college degree (64 percent), and white evangelical Christians (77 percent) (Pew Research Center 2018b; CNN 2016; Huang et al. 2016).

As the demographic profile of the United States continues to change and white people continue to decline as a share of the population (U.S. Census Bureau 2017a), the Republican

Party faces an existential dilemma: at some point there will simply not be enough old, white, evangelical men for them to win elections. This is why we have seen the aggressive rise in Republican-led voter suppression strategies (discussed below).

Our low overall rates of voting are often attributed to apathy: people just don't care enough to go to the trouble of fulfilling their duties as citizens, the argument goes. But there are better explanations, many of which recognize that voting is more difficult in the United States. Unlike in many other nations, election day is not a holiday, and it is not even on a weekend, posing particular challenges for people who work on the Tuesdays when we typically cast ballots. (More states had been moving to voting by mail and extended "early voting" periods, and even more did so during the 2020 pandemic election, but these are among the innovations that have been under attack.) The registration process creates hurdles, too. Many states require that people register up to thirty days prior to a given election, which especially affects transient populations. You might expect that political parties would work consistently to increase voter registration and participation, but historically they have done so only when they were reasonably certain that they could predict the effects of new voters entering the system and that they would benefit. At the same time, both major parties have worked to structure state-level ballot-access rules to limit the ability of third parties to gain a foothold, fearful of the effects on their electoral success (Piven and Cloward 2000).

Although the U.S. Constitution does not require (or even mention) registration, it does delegate to states the ability to determine "the time, places, and manner of holding elections"

(Article I, Section 4). The result, as with so much of our "federated" system that scatters authority across multiple levels of government, is rules, regulations, and procedures that differ widely from state to state and even from jurisdiction to jurisdiction within states. By one estimate, there were 10,500 separate entities responsible for carrying out the 2020 elections across the country (Hasen 2020). With different voting hours, registration deadlines and rules, voter identification regulations and standards, and methods of voting (hand-marked and hand-counted paper ballots; electronic touch screens; optically scanned "bubble-fill" forms; punch cards; mail-in ballots with complicated signature, witness, or notary requirements; and so on), along with shifting polling places, is it any wonder that people do not always know when, where, or how to vote? Or that less educated and more time-constrained people are more likely to be so frustrated with or alienated by the process that they just give up? Predictably, people who were eligible to vote in 2016 but did not do so were more likely to be poor, young, less educated, and nonwhite (Pew Research Center 2018b).

Because of disenfranchisement laws that operate in every state except Maine and Vermont, more than 5.1 million people were prohibited from voting in 2020 because of a felony conviction; in eleven states, that was true even for some of those who had served their sentence and completed probation or parole. Because of these laws, one in sixteen African Americans has lost the right to vote (Uggen, Shannon, and Pulido-Nava 2020). Moreover, the census counts prisoners as being residents of the location where they are imprisoned, not where they come from (Prison Policy Initiative 2020); because prisons are often located in rural areas, this is yet another source of regional/geographic bias (benefitting, at this time, Republicans and whites).

All of this variation has been made worse by the 2013 Supreme Court decision in *Shelby County v. Holder*, which weakened the 1965 Voting Rights Act (VRA), making it easier for states with histories of racist voting practices to implement laws and procedures that disenfranchise Black and brown citizens. Aided by *Shelby*, but accelerating activity that had begun long before, Republican-led state legislatures have enacted rule changes that create yet more obstacles to voting, such as photo ID laws and heightened proof-of-residency requirements, coupled with purges of the registration rolls, cuts to early-voting hours, and reductions in the number of voting machines in selected districts. Between 2012 and 2018, a total of 1,688 polling places were closed in counties now no longer protected by the VRA, thanks to *Shelby* (Leadership Conference Education Fund 2019). Since 2010, twenty-five states have passed new laws that, in one way or another, create obstacles, or administrative burdens, to voting (Herd and Moynihan 2018; ACLU 2020; Brennan Center for Justice 2019); another 361 such bills were introduced in forty-seven states in the first three months of 2021 (Brennan Center for Justice 2021). These are typically instituted in the name of preventing in-person voter fraud, but the weight of research on the topic shows that this is simply not a problem of any scale or scope (Brennan Center for Justice 2017). The myth of voter fraud (Minnite 2010) is a tactic used to justify laws designed to stop the groups of people who are most likely to vote Democratic from being able to vote at all.

There are material consequences to all of this. Take the time required to vote. As one 2019 report noted, "long wait times [are] more likely to occur in precincts with high minority populations, high population density, and low incomes." Wait times are also longer in places with more renters than home-owners. According to Census Bureau data, long lines may have caused as many as 560,000 eligible voters not to vote in 2016, and other research suggests that long waits experienced in the election of 2012 caused some 200,000 people not to try to vote two years later in 2014 (Weill et al. 2019). Or consider absen-tee and mail-in voting. In the 2016 election, almost 320,000 ballots were rejected for one reason or another—because the ballot didn't arrive by the deadline, it was missing a signature, the signature was deemed not to match that on file, it lacked a witness's signature, and so on (U.S. Election Assistance Com-mission 2017). In the primary contests of 2020, the number of ballots rejected was nearly 560,000 (Fessler and Moore 2020); the evidence about rejected ballots in the 2020 general election is mixed (Ballotpedia 2020d; Rakich 2021).

While some 15 percent of voters who were registered but did not vote in 2016 told a Census Bureau survey that it was because they were "not interested," and another 25 percent said that they "did not like candidates or campaign issues," some 12 percent cited illness or disability, 14 percent pointed to conflicts with their schedule, and more than 4 percent cited problems with the registration process (U.S. Census Bureau 2017b). The last three categories amounted to 5.7 million potential votes. Even among those who replied "not interested" or "don't like the candidates or issues" are surely people who are not necessarily apathetic but who don't vote because they have not seen their lives, or those of their family, friends, and neighbors, get better. So why should they go to considerable effort, and maybe even lose income, to show up at the polls (Piven and Cloward 2000)? As we will see in chapter 13 when we look at the responsiveness of Congress to people's wants and needs, this reaction may be justifiable; and as chapter 11 shows, government programs and institutions that treat people badly teach them lessons about their value as citizens and demobilize them. In sum, voting rates are lower among more vulnerable populations because policies and practices are designed to achieve that outcome.

The Constitution does not include an affirmative right to vote. Instead, the Constitution has added limits on the reasons one can use to deny access to the franchise: The Fifteenth Amendment made it illegal to restrict voting on the basis of race; the Nineteenth Amendment forbids discrimination on the basis of sex; and the Twenty-Sixth Amendment prohibits denial of the franchise on the basis of age for those over eighteen. But the Fifteenth Amendment was ignored throughout the South during the Jim Crow era, and states imposed poll taxes, literacy tests, grandfather clauses, and other measures designed to prevent formerly enslaved people and their descendants from voting (Keyssar 2009); those rules were enforced through campaigns of violence and terror by vigilantes like the Ku Klux Klan to ensure that the message was made clear (Equal Justice Initiative 2017). More recently, the Trump administration engaged in an increasingly bold effort to sabotage and overturn the 2020 presidential election, making arguments and filing lawsuits that had the effect of suggesting that only votes in predominantly white places should be counted (Summers 2020).

LESSONS FOR PRACTICE

The populations that are most likely to be our clients are the same populations that are the least reliable voters, and it is not coincidental that the policy-making system often ignores their needs. As a crude practical matter, why should it care about people who do not give it the two things it most needs: money and votes?

You can help in simple, straightforward ways. First, to risk stating what may be obvious, you should vote, and you should do so in each and every election, including those for school board, zoning commission, sheriff, and members of the state legislature, as well as in the presidential and congressional elections that tend to get all the attention. Along with that, make sure that your neighbors, colleagues, and clients are registered and that they vote too. Reach out to your friends: Are they registered? Do they have a plan for voting? Can you help? Have you sent them a reminder message prior to election day? There's emerging evidence that friend-to-friend texting can be among the most effective strategies for increasing turnout (Schein et al. 2020).

To reach others, you can conduct nonpartisan registration drives and then engage in get-out-the-vote activities. Send texts, make phone calls, go canvassing door-to-door, distribute yard signs, drive people to the polls, or volunteer to be a ballot clerk on election day. This kind of labor can be especially valued and have a greater impact on those local elections that many people ignore. So reach out to your local political party or to local campaigns—they can always make use of a committed volunteer, especially one with knowledge and skills. As we will see, voting is not enough, but it is a simple first step and the foundation of any democratic system. It's an easy and important place to begin.

Finally, if you want to focus your advocacy on bigger, harder, and longer-term solutions, look for organizations that are working to advance a constitutional right to vote that would, in one election scholar's formulation, "guarantee all adult citizens the right to vote in federal elections, establish a nonpartisan administrative body to run federal elections that would automatically register all eligible voters to vote, and impose basic standards of voting access and competency for state and local elections" (Hasen 2020).

Chapter Four

WE ARE EXCEPTIONAL—BUT NOT IN A GOOD WAY

GIVEN WHAT we have seen in the preceding chapters about the ways the U.S. system is undemocratic, the number of people it excludes from its most basic civic activity, and how it fails to represent majority interests, it may make sense that our system also fails to ensure the well-being of the majority in ways that other rich democracies do.

According to recent data, of the thirty-seven member nations of the Organization for Economic Cooperation and Development (OECD), only three had higher rates of overall poverty than the United States (Brazil, Costa Rica, and South Africa), only six had higher rates of child poverty (Chile, Israel, Romania, Turkey, Costa Rica, and South Africa), and only six had higher rates of income inequality (Bulgaria, Turkey, Mexico, Chile, Costa Rica, and South Africa) (OECD 2020a). Compared to the OECD average, we have lower life expectancy, higher unemployment rates (but with more hours worked by the employed), higher health-care costs (yet more people without access), and fewer people with old age pensions. We also have a smaller share of women in the national legislature, as we've seen, plus a lower share of energy provided by renewable sources and higher rates of CO_2 emission (OECD 2020b).

Compared to ten other high-income countries (Australia, Canada, France, Germany, the Netherlands, New Zealand, Norway, Sweden, Switzerland, and the United Kingdom), we have the lowest life expectancy; not coincidentally, we also have the highest rates of obesity, suicide, chronic disease burden (having two or more conditions like arthritis, high blood pressure, asthma, and heart disease), and avoidable death (Tikkanen and Abrams 2020). Our infant mortality rate is higher than that of forty-four other countries (World Bank 2020), and our maternal mortality rate (the number of women who die in pregnancy or from childbirth) is higher than that of fifty-four countries— the highest among the world's rich democracies (Belluz 2020). These rates are two to three times higher for Black and Native women than they are for white women (Centers for Disease Control 2019).

In rich democracies, including the United States, we expect that in the modern era life expectancy will rise and mortality rates will decline over time. But since 1999, we have seen an increase in "deaths of despair"—from suicide, drug overdose, and alcohol-related liver disease—among middle-aged non-Hispanic whites, especially those with a high school education or less, even when rates have continued to fall for other groups (Case and Deaton 2015, 2017). We see this play out in other research that seeks to measure people's self-reported happiness (there is in fact a branch of scholarship called Happiness Studies); that research finds that the happiest people in the world live in Finland, Denmark, and Switzerland. The United States ranks eighteenth (Helliwell et al. 2020).

Perhaps this is because, contrary to the story that we tell ourselves and the world about who we are, the United States is not a land of widespread opportunity. There are twelve countries in which it takes fewer generations for children born into a low-income family to reach the middle class; that is, there is more upward mobility in the Netherlands, Japan, Australia, Belgium, Greece, Canada, New Zealand, Spain, Sweden, Finland, Norway, and Denmark (OECD 2018). In the United States, the best predictor of what your income will be when you become an adult is not how hard you work but what your father's income was (Hipple 2019; Corak 2016). In that way we have a more rigid class structure than the UK, which still has a monarchy and hereditary titles. Most children born in the United States would do better if they were born elsewhere, unless they got lucky and were born to the right parents. This is often hard for people to hear because it challenges what is perhaps our core national narrative—that anyone who works hard and plays by the rules can grow up to be anything they want to be, that we offer greater opportunity here than other countries do, that we are a meritocracy. The data tell us that's not true.

We can see this clearly if we consider two ways of measuring poverty. One is to examine how much poverty the market creates: how many people are poor prior to anything the government might do to relieve it. This is sometimes called the pre-transfer poverty rate or the market poverty rate. On this measure, the United States does not look like much of an out-lier; in fact, we have lower pre-transfer poverty rates than France, Germany, Australia, and even Sweden, and about the same rate as the Netherlands and the UK (Dutta-Gupta 2011). But notice what happens when we look at the post-transfer poverty rate, or how much poverty remains when we factor in the effects of all the things government does to reduce it. It is here that we see the "American exception." In other rich nations, many of which start out with more poverty created by the economy, government intervention cuts poverty significantly, bringing the "real" pov-erty rate down to 5 percent in Denmark and Sweden and 7 per-cent in Norway, France, Iceland, and Finland. But in the United States, when we factor in the effects of our welfare state, poverty is still at 17 percent (Dutta-Gupta 2011). Social welfare policy in France reduces poverty by 25 percentage points; in Germany, by 24 percentage points; in Finland, Belgium, and Italy, by 22; in the UK, by 20; in the Netherlands, by 17; and so on. At the bottom of the list, U.S. tax and transfer policies only bring down poverty by just under 10 percentage points (Gould and Wething 2012).

Put simply, we have more poverty because we do less to reduce it.

It's not just that the U.S. government does less to actively help people thrive; it has a much more fully developed repres-sive side than do other rich democracies. We came to occupy what we call "our" land through acts of genocide and forced relocation; built our economy in significant measure on the backs of enslaved people; used state-sanctioned violence to enforce racial apartheid, supplemented with official policies of discrimination (like redlining and restrictive covenants). In the post–World War II period, we built a fairly elaborate welfare state (see discussion of the G.I. Bill in chapter 11), but the benefits went mostly to whites; they got a leg up from government, with free college, health care, and low-cost housing, while those who were Black, Indigenous, and people of color (BIPOC) got a boot on their necks. Political scientist and historian Ira Katznelson refers to this as the period "when affirmative action was white" (Katznelson 2006).

Today, as a legacy of these racist, repressive systems, we incarcerate a larger share of our population than any nation in the world; in fact, we have so many people under the supervision of the criminal punishment system—people who are disproportionately Black and brown—that if every U.S. state were a separate country, twenty-three of them would still have the world's highest incarceration rate (P. Wagner and Sawyer 2018). Moreover, as of 2019, the United States was one of only twenty countries—among them, China, Iran, Saudi Arabia, Iraq, and Egypt—that used execution as a form of punishment (Amnesty International 2020); that practice also has a clear racial bias (Phillips and Marceau 2020). Whether we are talking about local governments hiring private Pinkerton detectives to shoot strikers and protesters in the nineteenth century (Churchill 2008) or the frequency with which armed agents of the state still kill people, especially Black men, with impunity (Tate, Jenkins, and Rich 2020), the violence government directs against us is not common in those other rich democracies with lower poverty and higher happiness indices.

People often attribute these differences to our political culture—the idea that there is something distinct about us, that our penchant for freedom, individual liberty, equality, and self-reliance has caused us to reject broad, expansive government interventions to improve collective well-being; we prefer a small, limited government, especially at the national level, and are content to have the private for-profit and not-for-profit sectors do things that in other places would be done by government. People do best, the argument goes, when they are more "free."

I do not find these cultural explanations persuasive. First, a child born into a lead-paint-riddled apartment near an incinerator in a neighborhood with a 40 percent poverty rate and regular double-digit unemployment, where the schools are dilapidated and underfunded and the water is unsafe to drink, is not "free" in any meaningful sense. To claim that limited government makes us freer is to raise the question: Who is "us"? And given the ways BIPOC have experienced U.S. state power, is it plausible to characterize our core ideology or experience as rooted in freedom and equality? Are the massive U.S. systems of incarceration and the hyper-policing of poor communities indicators of limited government?

The U.S. political tradition, with this history in mind, is as illiberal as it has been liberal (Smith 1993), and our history is at least as much one of defense of white power as it is of expansion of freedom and liberty. There is no one history of U.S. social welfare policy development and no single experience of the U.S. state. Instead, there are multiple histories that play out simultaneously along separate (sometimes overlapping or intersecting) paths. To be "American" has been a different experience for different peoples (C. Fox 2012; Pimpare 2007).

Donald Trump has perhaps done us a service in this regard. In the past, white people have found ways to convince themselves that the nation was at its core racially egalitarian, however imperfectly. But by saying the quiet parts out loud, by making subtext into text, and by turning racially coded dog whistles into racist bullhorns, Trump pierced this denial and helped people finally realize just how deeply racist the United States has been and continues to be. The sheer number of those previously in denial who joined in Black Lives Matter marches and protests is one small testament to that.

The second problem with pointing to our supposedly small-government political culture is that the usual claims about what policies and programs "individualist" and "antigovernment" people prefer are not borne out by the data. For about as long as we have been asking polling questions about policy preferences, majorities have typically said that it is government's responsibility to ensure that people have access to health care (Gallup 2007; Blendon and Benson 2001); throughout much of the twentieth century, they were also pretty consistent in their support for unemployment insurance programs, Social Security, publicly funded education, and even welfare and food stamps (Page and Shapiro 1982). Support for increasing taxes on corporations and higher-income people is consistently high, and many see paying taxes as an important part of their civic duty (Sawhill and Pulliam 2019). Perhaps people in the United States are "philosophically conservative but operationally liberal" (Drutman 2017). That is, the majority have policy preferences that are reasonably in line with NASW policy statements, and more people may agree with you on more occasions than you might think, but they simultaneously hold onto abstract ideas that do not correlate with their policy preferences; this would be consistent with what we know about people's general lack of political knowledge and their incoherent ideologies (see chapter 18).

There are other problems with cultural explanations. The core tenets of U.S. political culture are commonly understood to have remained essentially the same over time (freedom, individualism, limited government, self-reliance). But how can something static (these core features of political culture) explain something that has changed radically over the course of our history (social welfare policy and the size and reach of the state)? Finally, what is the causal mechanism? How does culture actually get made into policy? Think about Congress and lawmaking—how can we trace the effects of *culture* on the process? (Steinmo 1995).

A better explanation for our weak welfare state and for the dramatically worse outcomes so many of us confront lies in the structure and operation of those institutions described in previous chapters. When you consider our federal system (dividing power between the national and state governments), the bicameral legislature (requiring the House and Senate to agree, even when they are controlled by different parties), and the presidential veto power, we simply have more "veto points"—opportunities to stop change from happening—than do other long-standing democracies (Stepan and Linz 2011). There's also the U.S. federal courts' unusual power to overturn acts of the legislature and the uncommonly complex procedures for changing the Constitution. The result is a national policy-making system that requires extraordinary levels of cooperation; this has always been a challenge and helps explain why our two big "bangs" of national policy making (see the preface) came during periods of economic crisis and social unrest when there were also large Democratic supermajorities in Congress. Unlike in other systems, the impediments to change here are so great that it typically requires a "perfect storm" of conditions for major changes to be enacted. Add to all this our relatively weak and decentralized political parties and our enfeebled labor movement (in part because it was suppressed by state violence and because the federal-state division of power led to many separate state battles for worker rights and power instead of a single national one) (Steinmo 1995), and the case for our institutions rather than our culture as the best explanation for our exceptionalism seems strong.

LESSONS FOR PRACTICE

That's good news, in a way, because we know how to alter institutions (even if that is difficult), whereas how to change culture is still a bit of a puzzle.

Another lesson from this chapter is not to assume that people who are experiencing poverty are, at some level, responsible for it; that only makes sense (if even then) on the assumption that there really are abundant opportunities available to all and that we all, more or less, begin on a level playing field. But a child born to poor parents in a poor place might as well be born in an entirely different country than a child born under more favorable circumstances to parents with more money, education, and influence. One implication is that it is incoherent—and cruel—to attribute that child's poverty to their own behavior or moral failings; they exist in systems of oppression or elevation. As a consequence, solutions lie there, too—not in moral reform, therapy, admonitions to develop "grit," or entreaties to work harder. Indeed, another uncomfortable truth is that the nation is filled with people who work hard and do everything "right" and still remain stuck. Poor people don't need fixing, but our systems of access, opportunity, and support do. This is consistent with an ever-growing body of evidence that the most effective antipoverty program is not really a program at all: Just give poor people money and trust that they will know best how to spend it (Blattman et al. 2017; Martin 2019).

More generally, if you hear a behavioral or cultural explanation for something, pause and ask if there are other ways to make sense of the phenomenon under discussion. Are there structural forces at work? Systems of power and privilege? What systems are implicated, and how do they operate in practice? What kind of evidence would you need to see for such explanations to be persuasive? When you employ the person-in-environment theoretical framework, do you fully account for the ways environment can radically constrain an individual's opportunities for action?

Chapter Five

MOST OF US WILL BE POOR
AND ON WELFARE

SOMETIMES SOCIAL workers think of clients as "them," as a group that is separate from themselves, with distinct sets of problems that they do not or will not face. But this is not true, especially when we think of our poor and low-income clients.

According to the Census Bureau's official poverty measure (OPM), the poverty rate for 2019 was 10.5 percent; by the more sophisticated supplemental poverty measure (SPM), the rate was 11.7 percent (Semega et al. 2020; L. Fox 2020). These are point-in-time measures that tell us whose total income over the course of the year was at or below the official poverty threshold (about $26,000 for a family of four that year). But imagine this scenario: Your annual salary is $52,000, and you work from January through June; you are then unemployed and have no further income. Because your total income that year reached the poverty threshold ($26,000), the census counts you as not poor, even though you and your family went six months with no income whatsoever.

The Census Bureau knows that this is a problem, so they have periodically examined fluctuations in income over time. The most recent of these reports showed that over the two-year period from January 2013 through December 2014, 27.5 percent of the population had their income drop below the poverty line for at least two months (by contrast, the OPM for both years was 14.8 percent). This episodic poverty rate was 39.2 percent for African Americans, 40.9 percent for Hispanic Americans, 36.5 percent for children under the age of eighteen, and 51.5 percent for people in female-headed households (Mohanty 2019; U.S. Census Bureau 2020). Given that the episodic rate was 31.6 percent for the three-year period from 2009–2011 and 27.1 percent for the period from 2005–2007 (Edwards 2014), we might be better served by recognizing that the actual incidence of poverty in the United States is at least twice what the OPM or the SPM suggests.

The experience of poverty is more common than we think. Because so many of us have precarious incomes, perhaps just above the poverty line, all it takes is a single crisis (a broken-down car or an unexpected medical bill) to push a family's income below the poverty line; in time, most people are able to recover from the crisis and get their income back above the line again. But people's economic lives are fragile; official poverty measures understate that precarity (Kasmir 2018) and suggest that poverty affects far fewer people than it really does. Poverty is common in the United States, and economic insecurity is increasingly a defining characteristic of what it means to live in this country.

We see this still more clearly if we step back further to look at how many people experience poverty at any point during their lives. By that measure, the problem is even more widespread: 54

percent of U.S. adults will be poor for one year or more (measured at 150 percent of the OPM) (Rank, Hirschl, and Foster 2016); the rate of this life-course poverty for African Americans is 90 percent (Rank 2009). If we use relative poverty measures, instead of absolute threshold measures like the OPM or the SPM, the problem appears yet more acute. Over the course of our adult lives, 61.8 percent of us—almost two-thirds of the U.S. population—will see our income drop into the bottom 20 percent for a year or more; 42.1 percent of us will spend a year or more among the poorest 10 percent. What's more, 25 percent of us will suffer five or more years in the bottom fifth, and more than 11 percent will spend that long or longer in the bottom tenth (Rank and Hirschl 2015).

Our fortunes change over time. We are most vulnerable during those periods when we don't have access to money from the labor market—as children, in old age, after the birth of a child, or when we (or our family members) are sick or disabled (Rowntree 1901). And this is mostly how our largest social welfare programs—notably, Social Security—work: they transfer money from people who are working to those who are not. Throughout the life span, our role in that exchange relationship will shift, from being dependents (when we are children) to being workers to being dependents again (as we provide care for our children or parents or in our own old age). Of course, these patterns can be disrupted by changes in the economy or accidents of fate. Thus, over the course of our lives, some 14 percent of us will experience homelessness (Link et al. 1994), and more than 46 percent will experience one or more mental health disorders, as defined by the *DSM* (Kessler et al. 2005).

Because of this precarity, most of us will also benefit from one or more social welfare programs. In a 2012 Pew Research study, 55 percent of those surveyed reported having received benefits from Social Security, Medicaid, Medicare, SNAP, unemployment insurance, or AFDC/TANF; about one-third had benefited from two or more of those programs, and 15 percent from three or more. Moreover, 71 percent of all adults were in households in which someone had benefited from one or more of these programs (Morin, Taylor, and Patten 2012). In 2013, in the wake of the Great Recession, some 51 million of us were eligible for SNAP and 85 percent of that group received benefits—about 15 percent of the U.S. population (Rosenbaum and Keith-Jennings 2019).

Again, if we step back and look at how people experience government programs at different times in their lives, we find even broader need and more widespread use of them. Looking just at the means-tested programs—ones for which you must be poor enough to qualify—other research has estimated that 65 percent of all U.S. adults will at some point live in a household in which someone receives benefits, and 40 percent will do so for five years or more (Rank 2007). At its pre–Great Recession peak, the earned income tax credit (EITC) reached more than 16 percent of the population in a single year; the figure was 15 percent for Medicaid and 11 percent for food stamps (Mettler and Milstein 2007). Food stamps/SNAP have an especially broad reach: Half of us will at some point in our adulthood live in a household receiving those benefits, as will 40 percent of all children under the age of twenty. By the time we reach age sixty-five, 37.6 percent of us will have used a cash-assistance program and 65 percent will have used a cash or in-kind relief program (Rank 2007; Rank and Hirschl 2002, 2009). Not them—us.

All people everywhere are dependent; we are dependent on the state (government), the market (for labor income), and the family (for care and financial support). What distinguishes the United States from many other countries is that the structure of our social welfare state pushes us toward lodging our primary dependence in the labor market and limits our ability to shift that dependence to those other institutions. This is how one Danish sociologist taught us to evaluate welfare states in a more sophisticated manner: Rather than simply counting their spending, he argued, we should rank them by a standard of decommodification, or the extent to which they allow us to survive outside of dependence on the labor market (Esping-Andersen 1990). Subsequently, feminist scholars have added in the standard of defamilialization, or the extent to which the welfare state allows one to survive and thrive outside of dependence on a male breadwinner or the family more generally (O'Connor, Orloff, and Shaver 1999; Hernes 1987). On each of these counts, we fare badly.

Poverty in the United States is not something that happens to small numbers of people in unusual circumstances; it is a common experience. Indeed, it is this precariousness, this insecurity, that is increasingly a defining feature of what it means to live in the United States. This too is difficult for many people to accept, and it is hard to internalize, because it directly contradicts the stories that this country has been telling the world and itself about who we are.

LESSONS FOR PRACTICE

Don't talk about poor and low-income people as "them." If poverty has not already been part of your experience or your family's experience, recognize that the odds are high that it will be. In order to calculate your likelihood of being poor, go to confrontingpoverty.org/poverty-risk-calculator, a tool devised by Profs. Mark Robert Rank and Thomas A. Hirschl (Rank and Hirschl 2020). Are you surprised by what you find?

A basic principle of social work is that you meet the client where they are. This is true of policy analysis and advocacy too. You must diagnose the problem accurately but then deal with the actually existing opportunities for intervention—with the real system—rather than the one you wish were in operation. These chapters have unsettled some long-standing myths about the United States and revealed some uncomfortable truths, but our best hope for effecting change is to start with a clear-eyed appraisal of the nature of the challenges we all face and how vulnerable we all are made by this country's flimsy protections against accident and insecurity. As community organizer Saul Alinsky put it long ago, "As an organizer I start from where the world is, as it is, not as I would like it to be. That we accept the world as it is does not in any sense weaken our desire to change it into what we believe it should be—it is necessary to begin where the world is if we are going to change it to what we think it should be. That means working in the system" (Alinsky 1971).

Chapter Six

EVERYTHING IS POLITICAL

"I don't want to get political."
"We shouldn't politicize this."
"It's too soon to talk about the politics of this."
"It's not appropriate to politicize their death."
"Let's keep politics out of this."
"Never talk about politics or religion at the dinner table."

YOU HAVE probably heard some of these statements, or others like them, and perhaps even uttered them yourself. In all kinds of contexts, people encourage us to keep politics out of things, as if politics exists in its own separate space and can be cordoned off, somehow making human relations easier to manage. But even when it is not an outright effort at shutting down dialogue and debate, this is a fool's errand. Everything is political: politics is the way we make people aware of problems, introduce ideas into the public sphere, create frameworks for thinking about issues and their relative importance, structure debates about policy, frame defenses of justice and fairness and equity, and build consensus for change. Politics is how we improve the lives of our clients, our families, our friends, and our communities; it is the "contest where some gain the authority to make decisions of fundamental significance for others" (Hacker and Pierson 2014). Only if you don't care who has that decision-making authority should you want to avoid politics.

People sometimes discourage discussions about political issues because they want to evade confrontation. But it is precisely when people most disagree that it is most important to engage, because in sorting out our priorities and preferences for what governments should and should not do and for whom, we declare our values. Only then can we effectively prepare a strategy for winning majorities to effect change. Especially in the current period of hyperpolarization (in which there is little agreement between those who identify as Republicans and those who identify as Democrats), people may be especially wary, but to "get political" is to describe the world as it is and then imagine the world as you would like to see it. To recoil from political conversation, statements, and value making is to surrender power to others and to abandon your clients.

You will also hear complaints that one should not talk politics in the wake of a tragic event. After a mass shooting in a school, for example (now a regular occurrence in the United States), you will hear people say that it's improper to talk about gun safety and regulatory policies. That's exactly wrong: the immediate aftermath of such an event is precisely the moment to talk about these things. If you wait, as people will urge you to do (often, of course, it's the people who don't want to see policy changes), the time when people are really paying attention will have passed, and you will have lost an opportunity to advance the issue—or, to use the more formal language, to take advantage of an open "policy window" (Kingdon 2011). Insisting that the politics of an issue should not be discussed is itself a political claim.

Likewise, after the death of a famous political figure you will hear calls to "respect the dead and their family" and not talk about the harm they might have caused during their lives. Again, this strikes me as perfectly incorrect. When a powerful person has died and attention is being paid to their public life, what better time to examine its impact, good and bad?

Something similar is at work when people call for civility or accuse someone of being uncivil. This too is often a way to shut down uncomfortable speech, to close off discussion and debate, a way to preserve power and the status quo. Just as admonitions to avoid politicizing an issue are often an exertion of power and an effort to constrain debate, pleas for "civility" are often actually a plea for people not to say true things out loud. To be clear, I'm not talking about being rude, hijacking conversations, engaging in spittle-flecked tirades, or using whatever power you may have to punch down rather than up. What I *am* saying is that calls for civility are often a disguised attempt to delegitimize speech that challenges existing allocations of power and authority. Don't fall for it.

U.S. House member Ilhan Omar, a Black, Muslim, immigrant woman representing Minnesota's Fifth District, put it this way: "People will say it's my 'tone.' I'm like, you're agitated by my tone because you think people like me should be sitting in a corner, not heard and not seen. Everything that comes out of my mouth is going to be filtered through the lens of you despising my existence" (Marchese 2020).

Moreover, if what we are talking about is, say, the forced separation of migrant families and the caging of children in concentration camps (Soboroff 2020), the routinized assault and murder of Black people at the hands of the police (Tate, Jenkins, and Rich 2020), widespread poverty and hunger (Alston

2017; Pimpare 2008), or an attempted coup by a white national-
ist president (*autogolpe* is the formal term for Trump's effort to
retain power despite his defeat at the polls), then "uncivil" dis-
course may actually be the most appropriate reaction, especially
from social workers, who have an obligation to fight on behalf
of marginalized populations and to advance social justice. If you
are being told that you are radical, unrealistic, angry, or disre-
spectful, it is possible that you are, in fact, on the right track
and saying things that need to be said. What the "tone police"
are reacting to is their discomfort at being called to account;
they are hoping to shame you into allowing them to continue to
perpetuate injustice. Calls for civility are ways for people with
power to portray themselves as victims and to avoid being criticized or held responsible for their action or inaction.

The Rev. Martin Luther King, Jr. (1963) offered particularly
apt words in his "Letter from a Birmingham Jail":

> I have almost reached the regrettable conclusion that the
> Negro's great stumbling block in his stride toward freedom
> is not the White Citizen's Counciler or the Ku Klux Klanner,
> but the white moderate, who is more devoted to "order" than
> to justice; who prefers a negative peace which is the absence
> of tension to a positive peace which is the presence of justice.

Abolitionist Frederick Douglass (1857) was on point here as
well:

> Power concedes nothing without a demand. It never did
> and it never will. Find out just what any people will quietly

submit to and you have found out the exact measure of injustice and wrong which will be imposed upon them, and these will continue till they are resisted with either words or blows, or with both.

Finally, we could listen to political scientist E. E. Schattschneider ([1960] 1975, 68):

Political conflict is not like an intercollegiate debate in which the opponents agree in advance on a definition of the issues. As a matter of fact, *the definition of the alternatives is the supreme instrument of power*; the antagonists can rarely agree on what the issues are because power is involved in the definition. He who determines what politics is about runs the country, because the definition of the alternatives is the choice of conflicts, and the choice of conflicts allocates power. It follows that all conflict is confusing.

LESSONS FOR PRACTICE

I have something of a reputation as being the person in the room who will say out loud what other people are thinking but no one wants to voice. It's not unusual, if I am raising a direct question to a person in authority, for the person to laugh a bit uncomfortably and say, "Well, I wouldn't put it quite like that." It's a way of saying "When you state clearly and plainly the implications of what I am suggesting, it sounds just as bad as it is. It's rude not to let me get away with language that obscures the real impact of my position." In an ideal world there is always someone in the room who is willing to challenge authority and speak plainly; because I am a middle-aged white man with a PhD, I can get away with a lot more of this than many other people could. It's a small way I can use the power that I have on behalf of others who might not have the same ability. If you too are in that position, think about how to use your own power effectively in service to others.

And remember: Everything is political.

Chapter Seven

CONSERVATISM IS NOT CONSERVATIVE AND SOME OF US ARE MORE POLARIZED THAN OTHERS

CONSERVATIVES WOULD tell you that the heart of their philosophy is a belief in limited government, born of the conviction that state power is a threat to both individual liberty and personal property. "That government is best which governs least," as Henry David Thoreau put it (Thoreau [1849] 2017). Their rhetoric often privileges moderation above all, holding up preservation of the status quo and resistance to change, especially quick change, as a way to safeguard freedom.

Political theorist Corey Robin (2018) has argued that the story that conservatives tell about who they are and what their core values are—going back to British member of Parliament Edmund Burke, a founder of modern conservatism—doesn't accurately describe either their ethos or their actions. Rather than being conservative, they are *reactionary*, Robin contends: Conservatives (and today's Republicans) hold as their true core value the preservation of political, economic, and social power in the hands of propertied, straight-identified, white men, and the history of their movement has been their consistent opposition to extending power and influence to other groups—women, people of color, LGBTQ people, and so on. The history of the United States is, in many ways, a history of the fights to expand rights to groups that have been excluded, and that does indeed come at the expense of those who were used to having a monopoly on power and resources. Indignant and angry at having to share, these white men and their accomplices have fought such inclusion at every turn (Anderson 2017; Cordova 2020; Hughey 2014; Mutz 2018). *Revanchism* is another word for a political program whose core mission is to recoup lost status or power.

This is perhaps why the movement broadly, and Trump specifically, can seem juvenile (Drezner 2020): at heart their main complaint is that they don't want to share. They have convinced themselves that they alone are fit to govern, either out of divine right or just deserts. This unwarranted sense of entitlement coupled with anger and fear that others are usurping the monopoly they have enjoyed over most of Western history helps explain why Trump, and the modern Republican Party, is angry, arrogant, and ignorant all at once (Craig and Richeson 2017).

But it is dangerous, too, as we saw with the right-wing attack on the U.S. Capitol in early 2021. For some time now, experts have been trying to warn Congress and the nation of the rise of domestic white supremacist terrorism and its troubling ties to law enforcement (FBI Counterterrorism Division 2006; Perliger 2012; Chermak, Freilich, and Suttmoeller 2011; U.S. Department of Homeland Security 2009, 2020). What is the "Make America Great Again" slogan, after all, but a call to return to some mythic period in which domination of the political, social, and economic systems by white men was ordinary (Eddington 2018; Mutz 2018).

Trumpism, like conservatism, is thus interested not merely in maintaining a status quo but in rolling back the advances of the twentieth century. It also serves as a useful reminder that history does not move only in one direction and that progress can be followed by regress. This is the lesson of the United States in the wake of the Civil War. During the period of Radical Reconstruction, in which troops from the North occupied the South to enforce the outcome of that bloody conflict, some two thousand Black men, many of whom had been enslaved, would hold local, state, and federal office—including in the U.S. House and Senate; in fact, from 1869 to 1901, every Congress but one had at least one Black member. But once those troops were withdrawn as part of the corrupt bargain to resolve the contested election of 1876, the Democratic South sought once again to deny these basic rights to Black Americans, who would not again occupy public office in nontrivial numbers until after the passage of the Civil Rights Act of 1964 (Foner 1993; Mettler and Lieberman 2020), by which time the Democratic Party had switched sides to become advocates of civil rights while the Republican Party became their chief antagonist.

Trump was not the problem but a symptom of a much deeper disease. As political scientists Jacob Hacker and Paul Pierson put it, "Trump turned the dial to eleven, but he did so on a machine that was already built" (Hacker and Pierson 2020, 4).

There are really two problems. One is that the Madiso-
nian system itself clearly cannot function as intended in an
era of strong, hyperpolarized parties. Those parties have grown
further and further apart over the past decades, although the
Republican Party has moved much further right than the
Democratic Party has moved left (Bonica et al. 2013; McCarty
2019; Ingraham 2020b; Mann and Ornstein 2016). That's part of
the "asymmetric" nature of our period of asymmetric polarization. So too is the fact that Democratic voters are much more
likely to value compromise than are Republican ones (Newport 2017). In fact, today's Republicans are among the most
right-wing parties in any rich democracy (Chinoy 2019; Lührmann et al. 2020), and Trump was representative of that, not
an aberration, as even a growing number of Republicans and
assiduously nonpartisan observers have come to concede (Stevens 2020; Mann and Ornstein 2016). What this polarization
means in practice is that a system that counts on Congress to
defend its powers and fight to limit the encroachments of the
executive branch will fail if members of Congress defend their
party's interest instead the institution's interest or the interests
of the nation. All of this is exacerbated by our increased tendency toward affective polarization, in which the other political party is seen not merely as the opposition but as the enemy
(Iyengar et al. 2019; Finkel et al. 2020). This was not the case
when the Democratic Party was rife with conservative (mostly
Southern) members and the Republican Party had an ample
supply of (Northern) liberals. But now the parties have "sorted"
themselves ideologically and stand more firmly in consistent
opposition.

The second problem, and a related one, is that one of those parties, because it has embraced racism, xenophobia, misogyny, and homophobia, faces increasingly poor electoral chances as its core message appeals to a smaller and smaller share of the population. Because the Republican Party has been unwilling, at least so far, to alter its commitments to appeal to more people (George W. Bush was arguably the last national Republican to really try), it has been left with one alternative: Alter the rules of the game, rig elections and processes, bend and break rules, lie to voters about its real agenda, and cheat (Keyssar 2012; Hacker and Pierson 2020). This highlights one of the challenges of this era: To accurately describe what we know to be true from the best available data and research is to sound partisan. But in the words of satirist Stephen Colbert, "Reality has a well-known liberal bias" (WHCA 2006).

Increased gerrymandering is a part of the problem, but only a part. Every ten years the country is supposed to conduct a full count of all the people here and where they live—this is the census that is required by the Constitution (Article 1, Section 2). Among other things, this determines how many representatives each state gets in the U.S. House (since its total number has been capped at 435 since 1929). The more people in a state, the more House members it is entitled to. Because people move and populations change, after the census some states will lose representatives and some will gain (although each state must have at least one House member to go along with its two senators); thus, the House must be reapportioned. Once the clerk of the House determines how many House members each state will get (Eckman 2019), each state legislature then decides how to draw the districts that each member will represent; whichever party controls that state's legislature will dominate this process, except in the ten states that have established nonpartisan commissions for this purpose (Ballotpedia 2020a). You have likely seen pictures of weirdly shaped congressional districts; they are shaped like that because legislatures design districts in a way that advantages the majority party, carefully constructing them so that just the right number of their supporters are in the district to guarantee a win for their own party while spreading out the other party's voters across as many districts as possible to dilute their influence. This is what is meant by gerrymandering, and it can be done with great precision (Newkirk 2017; Gupta 2020; Engstrom 2020), made easier by the fact that people tend to live near people like them; this last point is especially important because the consensus view is that this geographic sorting has more to with polarization than gerrymandering does (Dews 2017).

You will periodically hear people suggest that the answer to this is a third party—but none of those people are likely to be political scientists. As with term limits (see chapter 13), we are fairly united on this matter: The design of U.S. election systems does not afford meaningful space for third-party candidates to win office, with the occasional exception. This is Duverger's Law (G. W. Brown, McLean, and McMillan 2018), which says that in single-member districts, in which whoever wins the most votes gets the only legislative seat, there will only be room for two parties. Because you need to appeal to at least half of the population to win, smaller parties with narrower appeal cannot ordinarily succeed. This is unlike parliamentary systems with multimember districts, where a party can earn a seat with as little as 5 percent of the vote; the higher your party's share of the vote, the more seats you gain (Grote 2016; Kuca 2019). Nor can you get rid of parties entirely, despite the hope among the drafters of the Constitution that this would be possible (Aldrich 1995). Indeed, part of why the U.S. system has failed us so badly of late is that it was explicitly designed for a world in which there would be no parties, or "factions" as Madison called them (Hamilton, Madison, and Jay [1788] 1992).

Among other remedies for our hyperpartisan era, you might also hear paeans to "independents" and appeals to bring them more into discussion and debate in order to reach compromise. But there are relatively few genuinely independent voters. Although more people have identified themselves as "independent" or "unaffiliated" over the past decades, the majority of them are secret partisans—that is, they consistently vote along predictable party lines, even if they choose not be identified with the party they vote for (Pew Research Center 2019a). True independents are rare, and this may actually be a good thing: As we've seen, never have the two U.S. political parties been so effectively sorted; on almost any issue, you are likely to be able to identify what the Republican position is and what the Democratic position is. It should be easier than at almost any time in our history for voters to know whether their own views and preferences align more closely with Republicans or Democrats. This means that true independents, whose partisan loyalty can change from election to election or from office to office on the same ballot, tend to be among the least informed and most ideologically inconsistent and incoherent voters; they have not read the cues about which party is their logical home (Drutman 2019). If this is the case, then the less effort made to appeal to them the better, perhaps, especially given how uninformed even the more engaged voters tend to be (see chapter 13).

LESSONS FOR PRACTICE

Asymmetric polarization is a central feature of politics today—perhaps *the* central feature—and to treat both parties as essentially the same is to be in denial of the consensus that the problem is rooted in an increasingly radical, reactionary, insurgent Republican Party (Grossmann and Hopkins 2016; Fishkin and Pozen 2018; Pierson and Schickler 2020; Russell 2018; Thomsen 2014; Hacker and Pierson 2020; Mann and Ornstein 2016; Thurber and Yoshinaka 2015). Republicans have exploited the undemocratic aspects of the U.S. political system in an effort to enshrine their own minority rule in pursuit of a wildly unpopular agenda (Hacker and Pierson 2020), and to try to be "fair" by looking for ways to complain that "both sides" are to blame for the state of national politics today is to fail to take seriously their extremism and intransigence. This is not to argue, I hasten to add, that Democrats are without fault—far from it!—but the unresponsiveness of our national institutions to majority needs and desires is mostly a Republican problem in this era. To admit this is to sound biased, but you must make your peace with that. It is sometimes not possible to be truthful and evenhanded at the same time.

That said, keep in mind that the public is actually much less polarized than are party leaders and other elites (Fiorina, Abrams, and Pope 2011; Fiorina 2017), and there is often less true partisan division at the local level. As former New York City mayor Fiorello La Guardia supposedly once said, "There is no Democratic or Republican way of cleaning the streets." If the ugly state of national partisan politics is not for you (and I can understand why you might not want to immerse yourself in that world), then look for the political and policy spaces closer to you and find ways to develop your knowledge, networks, and actions in local politics. There will be more on that to come.

Chapter Eight

CRUEL AND UNJUST POLICIES SERVE A PURPOSE FOR SOMEONE

SOMETIMES SOCIAL workers can fall into the trap of thinking that their values are universal ones and that their goals of improving the well-being of vulnerable and marginalized populations are broadly shared. People living without adequate food, shelter, or health care are serious problems, we know, and if more people understood just how bad conditions are, they would be motivated to develop and implement solutions. But what you think of as a policy failure for your clients may be to someone's benefit, and when you say a policy "doesn't make any sense," it probably does—to someone else.

Take our unusually high incidence of poverty, which you might think everyone would define as a bad thing, even if some placed a lower priority on addressing it than others do. But poverty is advantageous to some groups and institutions. Sociologist Herbert Gans identified more than a dozen of these positive functions of poverty a generation ago. The continuing presence of poverty, he observed, ensures that there will be people desperate enough to do "dirty work," the unsafe, underpaid, undervalued labor that is often done by immigrants (think of meat-processing plants and agricultural work during the coronavirus pandemic). They also do the service-sector work that makes the lives of higher-income people easier (baristas, restaurant servers, housekeepers, nannies, Instacart shoppers, Uber drivers, and so on). Poverty makes possible a broad range of institutions and occupations, including police, prisons, pawn shops, check cashers, predatory for-profit colleges, and social work (not to mention the elaborate apparatuses of philanthropy and fundraising). And the presence of poor people bolsters the status of everyone above them in the economic and social hierarchy (Gans 1971, 1972). There's now extensive research that looks critically at not-for-profit social assistance programs and amplifies Gans's observation about the ways "do-gooder" professions, including social work, benefit from (and perhaps even perpetuate) poverty (Funiciello 1993; Poppendieck 1999; D. Wagner 2000; Polsky 1993; Giridharadas 2019; Spade 2020).

Frances Fox Piven and Richard A. Cloward identified the political functions of poverty and of relief programs. They argued that assistance to populations in need expands during times of social unrest in order to placate and disband unruly mobs (think of the "big bang" expansions in the wake of mass protest in the New Deal and Great Society eras) and then is cut back when "order" is restored to force poor people back out into the low-wage labor market (Piven and Cloward 1993). This way of thinking has something in common with Karl Marx's observation that capitalist systems depend on a "reserve army of labor," a steady supply of desperate people who will take any job available, which keeps wages low and workers compliant because there is always someone willing to do the work for less (Marx 1867). This is why business interests can reliably be expected to fight against programs of expanded public relief: the more one is able to secure some measure of economic stability from government, the more power one has to refuse degrading, unsafe, or poorly paid work (Pimpare 2004). While conservative thought typically asserts that an expansion of the welfare state leads to a reduction in liberty, the reality is that for many people living on the margins, access to reliable social welfare would make them significantly freer.

LESSONS FOR PRACTICE

If you confront a policy or a practice that you think is irrational, is badly designed, or generates unintended consequences that harm your clients, your neighbors, or other groups you care about or belong to, start by remembering the Latin expression *cui bono*—who benefits? Many (though not all) systems of discrimination and oppression serve someone's purpose. Think about what function they might serve and for whom. This is not to make you cynical, but to be clear-eyed about how to design an effective plan for changing bad policies and practices; if you begin from a place of naïveté and fail to comprehend the deeper functions of such systems, then the odds that you will succeed are sharply reduced.

Chapter Nine

WHERE YOU CAN GO DEPENDS ON WHERE YOU'VE BEEN

IT IS obvious to most people that politics creates policy: Knowing which party is in power, which interest groups are most mobilized, and which issues lawmakers choose to make a priority helps explain why particular laws are enacted (or not enacted) and the form that they take. The retirees' pension program in the Old Age, Survivors, and Disability Insurance program (OASDI) that we have come to call Social Security is a good example. How can we explain how and why this program was created in 1935? The nation was in a deep Depression that generated widespread need; pressure was mounting for relief for older people from the Share the Wealth and Townsend movements; there were historically large Democratic majorities in the House and the Senate (along with a Democratic president in FDR); Secretary of Labor Frances Perkins, a fierce advocate for the program, had influence over the president; and there was a growing recognition that enabling older workers to retire would open up scarce jobs for younger people (Downey 2009; Rauchway 2008).

But it is perhaps less obvious that policies create their own politics. Take Social Security again as the example of this "policy feedback" phenomenon. How do we explain why it came to be known as the sacrosanct and untouchable "third rail" of U.S. politics and why the George W. Bush administration's efforts to privatize it were so soundly defeated? Prior to the advent of Social Security, older people were among those least likely to vote; now they are the most likely, in part because Social Security gave them the time and the money to be engaged. It also gave them something important to defend, creating a personal and profound stake in politics and policy making. All of this is both cause and consequence of the formation of one of the most formidable interest groups in the United States, the American Association of Retired Persons (AARP) (Campbell 2011). The very way the program was structured helped to make it politically powerful. Here is one summary:

> By basing the program on insurance principles, FDR shielded Social Security from conservative charges that it was welfare. By funding the program through earmarked payroll contributions, Social Security created a powerful sense among workers that they were entitled to benefits upon retirement. And by ensuring that Social Security was housed in a well-funded, expert agency, the Roosevelt administration laid the groundwork for a competently-run bureaucracy that could defend the program in Congress and in the public. (Hertel-Fernandez 2020)

And here is an excellent definition of policy feedback more broadly:

> In contemporary political science, the concept of policy feedback suggests that policies can transform the political landscape in ways that are far more fundamental and varied. Policies, in this view, are not just political objects; they are political forces that reconfigure the underlying terms of power, reposition actors in political relations, and reshape political actors' identities, understandings, interests, and preferences. Indeed, to explain policy outcomes, this approach suggests, one must often look to the political dynamics set in motion by policy actions at earlier points in time. (Moynihan and Soss 2014, 321)

Path dependence is another idea that might help us think more rigorously (and more historically) about the roots of policy and their resilience to repeal or retrenchment. As the example this time, take health care in the United States. If we were building a system from scratch, most health policy scholars and a growing number of practitioners would create some kind of single-payer system in which all people automatically had access to care; they would go to their providers for treatment, and those providers would bill a government program according to prearranged rules and rates. There is an almost infinite array of forms such a program might take, but there is widespread agreement that by adopting such a system—which, in many formulations, would abolish private health insurance—we could extend health care to more people, radically improve health outcomes, and actually spend less money than we do now (Cai et al. 2020; Woolhandler and Himmelstein 2019). A win-win-win scenario.

Why, when undertaking a large-scale reform of the U.S. health system that had as its goal expanding access and lowering costs, did the Obama administration not consider change of this magnitude (Hacker 2010)? Because any such proposal would have activated the for-profit health insurance and pharmaceutical industries in opposition to it, surely dooming it to failure given their influence. Together these industries spent $5 billion on lobbying the federal government between 1999 and 2018—about $233 million per year. No other single industry group, other than the finance, insurance & real estate sector, has spent more on political contributions in recent years than have the health industries, with a total of $288 million just in 2019–2020 (Wouters 2020; OpenSecrets.org 2020). Part of the complicated explanation for the failure of the Clinton administration's efforts at health reform is the opposition from the health insurance industry and other business interests that benefited from the status quo (Oberlander 2007; Donnelly and Rochefort 2012).

Just as the structure of Social Security created interests and political power relationships, so too has the structure of our health system created its own allocation of stakeholders, largely as a result of choices made in the mid-1900s. We developed a robust scheme of employer-provided care delivered through for-profit insurance companies—often because unions fought for that as a benefit—and then subsidized it through the tax code by allowing those health costs to be excluded from your taxable income. That policy created people and groups with a stake in keeping it in place, which points to another piece of the puzzle: Because unions in the past won access to health insurance for their members as part of their bargaining efforts, they have had less reason to fight for more universal programs (Hacker 2002).

Obama received criticism from the left wing of his party for what some saw as the insurance- and pharma-friendliness of the Affordable Care Act. Indeed, two of the central pillars of the ACA—the individual mandate, which required that everyone have coverage of some kind, and the public subsidies that helped low- and middle-income people buy insurance on the private market—were efforts to prevent the insurance industry from fighting against reform as they had when Clinton tried and failed to expand access to health care. The mandate and the subsidies ultimately wound up generating more than eleven million new customers for U.S. insurance companies in recent years (Centers for Medicare & Medicaid Services 2020a). And that was the intent. What many called a sellout was a practical and probably necessary compromise to minimize disruption to existing systems in a way that would have caused powerful beneficiaries of the status quo to work against change (Hacker 2010).

All of this is a long way of saying that once the United States made private health insurance companies key constituents in our health system, it put us on a particular path, and the further we move along that path the harder it is to deviate from it. This way of thinking about the structural and institutional obstacles to broad-based policy change is the reason many academic political scientists who associate themselves with this American

Political Development framework can be exasperated by those who underestimate the obstacles to more radical change, even if we share the ultimate goal. Many policy scholars, that is, see the virtue in Medicare for all (recognizing that that is an umbrella term for lots of different approaches that may mean different things to different people) but believe that an approach that spreads out disruption to the existing system over time is more likely to be enacted in the first place and more liable to survive in the long run. This is not a case of liberal versus radical, I would argue, but a difference between those who think about the "layering" and "stickiness" of institutions and the policies and politics created by those structures and those who do not. Not all paths are always open; not all policy choices are necessarily available; and not all new policies will be equally resistant to efforts to repeal them.

LESSONS FOR PRACTICE

The problem is not identifying ways to improve current policies. Pick any issue area—immigration, affordable housing, health care, gun safety, food insecurity, foster care, early childhood education—and you can find an abundance of carefully crafted reform proposals that are likely to have significant, measurable, positive effects (National Association of Social Workers, Wehrmann, and McClain 2018). The problem we confront is how to build political power to enact them and then how to design policies so that they are (1) resistant to efforts to undo them and (2) ripe for adaptation and expansion. Do not underestimate the obstacles. Politics is complicated, and there are deep structural impediments to many kinds of change, not least of which is the problem of agency capture, in which the industries that are supposed to be regulated by government are in charge of them—think of oil industry lobbyists or executives being appointed to senior positions in the Environmental Protection Agency, for example (Dillon et al. 2018). It's not enough to consider the internal logic of one policy design approach over another or the politics of the moment; you must think through how the policy will alter the politics of it over time and how you might protect it from those who will seek to hinder its effectiveness in the future. This applies to your thinking about policy changes to programs within your own agencies, too. Only by appreciating those impediments and acting strategically can you hope to succeed.

Chapter Ten

LOOK AT WHAT'S NOT HAPPENING

BECAUSE THE U.S. political system is so responsive to minority pressures and requires so much cooperation across so many spaces in order for policy to be enacted, we have a status quo bias—the system is set up to resist change, and it offers greater opportunities to thwart action than do most other political arrangements. Doing nothing is always much easier than doing something, even if that something enjoys widespread support.

This was referred to long ago as the "second face of power"— the power to keep things off the policy agenda (Bachrach and Baratz 1962). Put differently, "Some issues are organized into politics while others are organized out" (Schattschneider [1960] 1975). We need to pay attention to nondecisions as well as decisions and to those things that are organized out of active political consideration.

The implications of this capacity to thwart action have been referred to more recently as policy drift—the ability to alter the ways policies function (or don't) and how effectively they serve their intended purpose (or don't) by stopping the enactment of laws that would keep old policies functioning effectively rather than by enacting new laws (Galvin and Hacker 2020; Hacker 2005). This happens a lot, even though we don't generally pay much attention to it. Most lobbying activity seeks to stop change rather than to enact laws, one expansive recent series of studies argues (Baumgartner et al. 2009). As a result, a lot of the advocacy activity in Washington is invisible to most observers because the mark of its success is . . . nothing happening.

The federal minimum wage is a good example. Accounting for inflation, its value is 31 percent lower than it was in 1968; opponents of higher wages can count this as a success, but they have achieved this goal without enacting laws. Instead, they have successfully obstructed efforts to pass national-level laws to raise it—the last such increase was in 2009, setting it at the current rate of $7.25 per hour (Cooper, Gould, and Zipperer 2019). Some states have stepped into the gap and raised their own minimums, but twenty-one states have not (Economic Policy Institute 2020).

Thus, if you want to limit a policy's reach but do not want to face the political consequences of changing it (or cannot muster majority support to enact cuts or alterations), then all you have to do is be patient and block every effort at reform. As we have discussed, because our political system typically makes obstruction easier than lawmaking, this confers yet another advantage on a minority that seeks to impede the expansion of the welfare or regulatory state. It's another way the U.S. system is undemocratic.

Policy drift happens in other areas, too. Think of the labor laws created long ago for a manufacturing economy that haven't kept pace with the changing mix of occupations in the United States; the fading of defined-benefit pension plans (Galvin and Hacker 2020); the declining ability of a range of social welfare programs, such as AFDC/TANF, unemployment insurance, and food stamps, to protect people from economic risks (Hacker 2005; Mettler and Milstein 2007); and of course all the programs and policies common to other rich democracies that are still missing here, such as paid family and medical leave, universal health care, national prekindergarten and day-care programs, and so on. These all amount to a limited welfare state that is increasingly unequal to modern challenges, a state of affairs achieved thanks to obstruction by a minority rather than lawmaking by a majority.

LESSONS FOR PRACTICE

Perhaps drift is another principle that is usefully applied at the agency level. What are the things that are not happening in your program or your agency? What are the conversations that are not taking place? Who are the people who are not in the room? What changes are not being considered? What is being kept off the agenda, how, and by whom? Don't underestimate how much easier it typically is to do nothing than to do something.

Inaction may be frustrating and bad for your clients or your community, but recognize that at any given moment agency or civic leaders are often confronting a broad range of complicated problems, some of which may require urgent attention. Thus, if you want to effect change, you must appreciate the challenge in all its dimensions, be patient, and be strategic.

Chapter Eleven

PEOPLE LEARN LESSONS ABOUT THEIR VALUE FROM THEIR INTERACTIONS WITH GOVERNMENT AGENCIES

IT'S NOT just that policies bring into being the interests that will fight for or against them, as we've seen; interaction with programs and policies can also alter how people think of and feel about government and how they engage with it. Some programs, because of how they are designed and administered, foster civic engagement, and some discourage it; interactions with those programs affect not only clients' appraisal of the agency they are dealing with, but of the entire political system.

Suzanne Mettler demonstrated this when she was trying to understand why the World War II generation had such high rates of voting, volunteering, and joining local organizations: It was these veterans' experience of the government itself that explained their robust civic engagement. The Servicemen's Readjustment Act of 1944—what you may know as the G.I. Bill—offered honorably discharged veterans low-interest home loans, expansive unemployment benefits, and free tuition (plus a living stipend) to go to college, vocational training, or apprenticeship programs (they were also eligible for health care through the Veterans Administration Health System, which predated the G.I. Bill). Keep in mind that something like 80 percent of all adult men in this period were veterans. What Mettler found was that, all else being equal, a white male veteran who used the G.I. Bill "belonged to 50 percent more civic organizations and participated in 30 percent more political activities" than one who did not. Why? Because their experience with the program—its generosity, efficiency, ease of access, and positive effect on their lives, along with their sense that the benefits were a fitting recognition for their service and their sacrifice—taught them that "government was for and about people like them. . . . Beneficiaries responded by embracing the duties and obligations of active citizenship." These effects were most pronounced among those from low- and moderate-income backgrounds (Mettler 2002, 2005a, 106). What's especially striking is that Black veterans, even though they were unable to access benefits at the same rates as white veterans in apartheid America, were more politically involved across every dimension, from contacting elected officials to working for a campaign to running for office themselves. They were also much more likely to have engaged in protest than were Black veterans who did not use G.I. Bill benefits and more likely to protest than white veterans whether or not they had used benefits (Mettler 2005b). The G.I. Bill had powerful effects on fostering active and engaged citizenship.

Andrea Campbell discovered that similar civic learning was cultivated by Social Security and Medicare. As we saw previously, Social Security confers money and time, giving older people a reason to engage politically and the time and money to do it. Their experience of that program, along with Medicare (which provides health care for those sixty-five and older), produces its own kind of feedback loop: Generous programs create the incentive and the ability to engage in politics, with the result that no group gives more money or votes more reliably than older people; because they do, the system is responsive to them, resulting in a commitment to protect and expand the programs that made them active in the first place. The engagement effects are so powerful that, contrary to the pattern with other age groups, low-income seniors—because they are more dependent on these programs—actually participate at greater rates (voting, making donations, and especially writing letters) than do higher-income seniors (Campbell 2011).

But policies can create vicious cycles as well as virtuous ones. We've long known that the people most likely to vote in the United States are those who have higher levels of formal education and those who are more affluent. Poor people vote at much lower rates than others (Erikson 2015; Schlozman, Brady, and Verba 2020; Soss and Jacobs 2009), and AFDC recipients in particular are among those least likely to vote. Joe Soss has shown that this is not because of any particular character trait or mere lack of resources but a consequence of their interaction with the program itself. AFDC demobilizes and causes people to disengage because of the way it treats them; it teaches them that government is arbitrary and punitive and that asserting themselves is pointless. It teaches passivity and obedience. Clients then carry those lessons over to other arenas of politics—and generalize from this experience to all of government—resulting in their having even lower levels of engagement than others with similar income and demographic characteristics who did not encounter the welfare program. By contrast, Social Security Disability Insurance (SSDI), which has clearer rules and offers fewer opportunities for seemingly arbitrary street-level decisions, inspires less fear of retribution against those who appeal decisions or lodge grievances. As a consequence, clients of this program had more faith in themselves and a greater sense that their own activism and engagement could make a difference. As Soss puts it, "welfare policy designs are more than just government outputs. They are political forces that have important effects on the beliefs and actions of citizens" (Soss 1999, 376). SSDI empowered clients; AFDC disempowered them.

Although there is enough debate to be cautious about concluding too much with certainty, there is also evidence that universal programs in general foster more political engagement and social trust than do means-tested ones (Kumlin and Rothstein 2005; Mettler and Stonecash 2008). This would seem to be borne out by what we know of the U.S. experience. Programs teach people about government and about their value in the political system, and different programs teach different lessons to different populations.

Other research has found differences even among means-tested programs that have different "authority structures." If we place Temporary Assistance to Needy Families (TANF, AFDC's successor), Head Start, and public housing programs along a continuum, in which "the ability to participate in decision processes that affect [clients] and the ability to check arbitrary exercises of authority" puts TANF at the most repressive end, Head Start at the other end, and housing programs in the middle, we discover that people who did not depend upon any of these programs had the highest rates of voting, political participation, and civic participation. Head Start increased civic engagement among those who used one of the three programs, and TANF worked to reduce it, with even greater effects evident in the more paternalistic TANF programs (TANF rules vary from state to state, and often even within states) (Bruch, Ferree, and Soss 2010, 210–11). There was little discernible effect from housing programs. So, even among programs that only target poorer people, variations in their structure and people's experience of them can produce in recipients different conceptions of their role as citizens (Bruch, Ferree, and Soss 2010). Unsurprisingly, alas, these experiences vary by race and gender even within the same program, with Black women being especially likely to have negative experiences (Ernst, Nguyen, and Taylor 2013).

To state what should be obvious at this point, there is a pattern. Policy can engage people and help make them more active citizens, or it can demobilize them. Returning to a question we considered earlier: Why do poor people vote less reliably? Well, maybe it's because government creates policies that are designed to detach them from politics and civic life, or at least have the effect of doing so. That lack of participation creates yet more incentives for politicians and their staffs to ignore them and their needs. Rinse, repeat.

Just as encounters with punitive programs like AFDC and TANF have consequences, encounters with our exceptionally punitive criminal legal system have yet more pronounced effects.

Even minor encounters with police—whether or not they result in arrest—are associated with a reduced likelihood of voting, but the more serious the encounter, the greater the effects. Those who encounter this system are also less likely to contribute to a political campaign, contact an elected official, volunteer for a community organization, or report having trust in government more generally (Weaver and Lerman 2010).

Sarah Bruch and Joe Soss bring this kind of analysis to children's experience in school, showing that these are sites where young people learn about their place in institutions and their relationship to authority in a way that "cultivat[es] political withdrawal and mistrust of government among the most socially disadvantaged" (Bruch and Soss 2018, 38). Students are taught obedience to the authority that is represented by school police, and Black and brown students are cited as misbehaving and punished more than white students. The most stringent of these regimes of compliance and control are in poorer schools with higher proportions of Black students. The result? Lower rates of voting and trust in government—by about 20 percent—that correlate with their punitive experiences in school (Bruch and Soss 2018). We think of schools as teaching citizenship, but for many they teach a kind of anti-civics because of the experiential lessons they imprint upon their young charges. Once again different groups of people are taught different lessons about their place in the polity.

Taking advantage of the wide disparities in how Medicaid functions from jurisdiction to jurisdiction (not just between states but between counties within a state and even from clinic to clinic within a city), Jamila Michener has documented the demobilizing experience of interacting with that program. What she found is consistent with the research we have been reviewing: Medicaid beneficiaries overall were less likely than others to register, to vote, and to belong to any political organization or attend a rally, with significant geographic variation; beneficiaries in states that had recently reduced benefits were significantly less likely to be engaged on all fronts. Few beneficiaries fought back against what they thought were arbitrary decisions, fed by their low perceptions of their own status and by a conviction that they were "just another number." The exceptions were typically middle-income people who did not identify as Black (Michener 2018).

Understanding what this all means is crucial to thinking strategically about policy design and about disrupting or altering existing policies. Something we should add to the mix is what Anne Schneider and Helen Ingram refer to as the "social construction of target populations." In order to make sense of policy making, they argue, we need to think about the objects of the policy: How are they thought of by the public and by lawmakers—sympathetically or unsympathetically? And how much power and influence do they wield—are they weak or strong? This gives us four categories: Those who are strong with positive constructions (the elderly or veterans are among their examples; these are the Advantaged); those who are strong with negative constructions (the rich or cultural elites, the Contenders); those who are weak but positively constructed (children or disabled people, the Dependents); and those who are weak and negatively constructed (criminals, welfare recipients, or those with substance use disorders, the Deviants). Among other things, this helps us start to think through why powerful groups do not always get what they want and why weak groups sometimes do (Schneider and Ingram 1993). Notice how this also points to a feedback loop: Government creates punitive policies for poor people that make them disengage from politics and civic life, which then further weakens them in policy making because they are not a force to be reckoned with. Policy is created or not created, at least in part, out of these constructions, but policy, in turn, also creates those constructions, as we have now seen.

The political weakness of low-income people is in some respects a creation of government itself—a mark of the success of those who would channel government services away from the majority and concentrate them on their preferred minority. The more we disable government programs, cut benefits, impose bureaucratic mazes, reduce responsiveness and efficiency, and rhetorically denigrate the public sector as unable to function effectively, the less people perceive themselves as having a stake in it (in part because, in truth, they have a reduced stake in it), and thus the less they will fight on behalf of it. Thus, convincing younger people that Social Security will not be around for them (Newport 2019) becomes a self-fulfilling prophecy if we allow it to.

Some of these effects are unintended consequences of badly designed policies or policies that have been affected by policy drift (see chapter 10) and no longer function as they once did. But many of these burdens are built into programs to limit access to them and reduce their costs—acts of bureaucratic disentitlement (Lipsky 1984). The consequences are clear: One 2003 summary of the research found that of all those eligible for food stamps, only between 54 and 71 percent (depending on the study) actually received benefits; the take-up rate was 64 percent for rental assistance, 50 to 56 percent for SSI, and 45 to 70 percent for AFDC (Remler and Glied 2003). In 2018, only 22 percent of families living at or below the poverty line received TANF benefits (it was half that in some states) (Floyd 2020); in 2016, a mere 27 percent of the jobless received unemployment insurance benefits (Evermore 2019) whereas 84 percent of those eligible received SNAP in 2017 (USDA Food and Nutrition Service 2019).

LESSONS FOR PRACTICE

Think about the systems your clients encounter—the programs, rules, regulations, mountains of paperwork, and the street-level bureaucrats, like you perhaps, who administer them (Lipsky 2010). What lessons are they being taught about their value, and about government itself? Given the research discussed in this chapter, how should you expect those encounters to shape their internal efficacy and their sense of external political efficacy? What kinds of citizens are these systems making? How you engage with your clients will have political effects. As Yeheskel Hasenfeld put it, "every action taken on behalf of a client not only represents some form of concrete service, such as counseling a family or determining eligibility for welfare, but also confers a moral judgment about their social worth" (Hasenfeld 2000, 329). So, the next time you find yourself losing patience or getting frustrated with a client, consider this research before you respond, remembering that badly designed policies may cause them to behave in what appear to be irrational or irresponsible ways.

How they encounter you—and what meaning they make of that encounter—can affect whether they seek assistance in the future, as recent research exploring attribution theory in childcare subsidy programs has shown (Barnes and Henly 2018). It is worth noting that Black clients were most likely to report negative encounters; this is something we should keep in mind as we continue to learn about why voter turnout may be lower in poor communities of color. Indeed, the research reviewed in this chapter has particular application for social workers seeking to encourage their poor clients to be more politically engaged; the forces inhibiting their participation may be much greater than previously assumed, presenting new challenges for the mobilization of disenfranchised populations.

Here's the hopeful part: Mettler's research on the G.I. Bill shows us that the "reciprocal obligation" it fostered can be brought to bear to create a more just society with a more engaged citizenry. Programs can, by their very structure, embrace individualism and selfishness, or they can instead conceive of us as "members of a shared community to which we all have responsibilities and in which we are all interdependent" (Mettler 2005a, 166). What role will you play in this?

Chapter Twelve

THE PEOPLE WHO BENEFIT MOST FROM GOVERNMENT ARE MOST LIKELY TO CLAIM THEY DON'T BENEFIT AT ALL

COMPARED TO most other rich democracies, the U.S. has a limited welfare state: Our public health, pension, housing, and other social assistance and insurance programs together constitute a smaller portion of total expenditures and less of our overall economy (OECD 2020c). This is true as far as it goes, but it is misleading, because one of the things that distinguishes us is how much of our social spending is indirect and administered through the tax code rather than in more obvious, direct ways. Take housing, for example. The 2021 budget request for the entire Department of Housing and Urban Development, which includes federal public housing construction and maintenance and rental assistance programs like Section 8 vouchers, was projected to be $47.9 billion (and at least $1.8 billion of that was for administrative expenses) (U.S. Department of Housing and Urban Development 2020). The beneficiaries of these programs are poor and low-income people, since eligibility is tied to income.

By comparison, the United States was expected to spend $30.2 billion in 2020 through the home mortgage interest deduction (Joint Committee on Taxation 2019). This provision of the tax code says that when you calculate your tax burden each April you can deduct from your income the interest that you pay on your home mortgage. The higher your mortgage, the larger your interest payments, and the more you get to deduct. The beneficiaries of this program are disproportionately higher-income taxpayers; in 2018, 90 percent of the benefits went to those with annual incomes over $100,000 (Tax Policy Center 2020).

Yet only the means-tested programs that reduce housing costs for poor people are generally thought of as social welfare, while the programs that lower the cost of housing for wealthier populations are barely even noticed at all.

Likewise, although we think of the $982 billion Social Security program as an important social-welfare resource (as we should), we are less likely to think of the provisions in the tax code that give preferential tax treatment to employer-provided pensions. Yet those are projected to cost $241.6 billion in 2020, and tax-deferred or tax-free IRA and Roth IRA retirement savings plans were expected to cost another $27.1 billion (Joint Committee on Taxation 2019). Because of the kinds of people who are likely to be employed in jobs that offer retirement plans and those who are likely to be able to save money in their own retirement accounts, these programs also benefit those with higher incomes.

Finally, we can note the preferential tax treatment granted to employer-provided health benefits, which were projected to cost $173.9 billion in 2020, while tax-free health savings accounts cost another $7.1 billion in lost revenue (Joint Committee on Taxation 2019). For comparison, spending on Medicaid, which disproportionately benefits lower-income people (although much of its spending is on older people in nursing homes) was $597 billion in 2018 (Centers for Medicare & Medicaid Services 2020a).

I am not arguing for or against these particular programs. What I am arguing, as others have before me, is that we should recognize these as government assistance programs and include them when we talk about the welfare state and who benefits from it. These other programs belong to what scholars have called the hidden welfare state (Howard 1997), the divided welfare state (Hacker 2002), or the submerged state (Mettler 2011). Christopher Faricy calls it "welfare for the wealthy" (Faricy 2016). You may have encountered a version of this argument—about the ways we underestimate the scope of the U.S. welfare state because of how we define "welfare"—in social work professor Mimi Abramovitz's classic article "Everyone Is Still on Welfare" (Abramovitz 2001).

Taken together, in 2018 the revenue surrendered to all tax expenditures was $1.4 trillion, greater than the amount spent on either Social Security ($982 billion) or Medicare and Medicaid ($971 billion). What's more, almost 60 percent of those tax expenditures went to the top 20 percent of earners, and 24 percent went to the top 1 percent (Center on Budget and Policy Priorities 2019).

Because so much government effort is hidden in this way, wealthier people are unaware of the ways they benefit from public programs, and as a result they systematically misunderstand what government does and for whom. In a cleverly designed research study, Suzanne Mettler found that fully 60 percent of those who benefited from the mortgage interest deduction said that they "have not used a government social program." The figure was 53 percent for those who received subsidized federal student loans and 64 percent for those who took advantage of tax-exempt 529 accounts to save for college. The consequences are significant. As she writes, "policies of the submerged state obscure the role of the government and exaggerate that of the market, leaving citizens unaware of how power operates, unable to form meaningful opinions, and incapable, therefore, of voicing their views accordingly" (Mettler 2011, 6). As we saw in chapter 11, the structure of policies and programs and how people interact with them can alter people's trust in government and their civic engagement. So, too, are there civic harms that come from so much of government activity being so obscure, because the ways it exacerbates inequality is also obscured. To take one dramatic example: In 2019, IRS tax audits of wealthy individuals and corporations declined to historic lows, while fully 39 percent of all audits were of recipients of the earned income tax credit (EITC)—people who, by definition, are working and poor—and the counties with the highest audit rates were disproportionately Black (Kiel 2020; Kiel and Fresques 2019).

However, Mettler also found that when people were informed about the distributional effects of programs—that the mortgage interest deduction mostly benefits wealthier people, for example—their opinions changed, with lower-income people voicing more disapproval and higher-income people voicing more approval. As she notes, another political scientist,

John Sides, discovered that when people were given accurate information about the estate tax and told how few people actually pay it—only the very wealthy—their support for it increased (Mettler 2011). While some political psychology research shows us how hard it is to change people's minds (see chapter 21), it's helpful to remember that there is also research that shows that it can in fact be done.

LESSONS FOR PRACTICE

What are the ways you and your family have benefited from the hidden welfare state?

The next time you hear someone complain about "welfare" expenditures or about how much money is spent on programs for poor and low-income people, find a way to share with them some of the information in this chapter. Let them know that the United States spends nearly as much money on housing subsidies to upper-income households as on lower-income ones or that we spend more money each year on tax breaks than we do on Social Security and Medicare. You can find a good collection of data, research reports, and graphics to share through the Tax Foundation (taxfoundation.org) and the National Priorities Project (nationalpriorities.org). We all benefit from the U.S. welfare state and therefore have a stake in it; part of our challenge is to make the hidden benefits more visible to those people who may not realize that they, too, are recipients of government assistance.

Chapter Thirteen

PEOPLE LIKE LICE AND COCKROACHES
BETTER THAN CONGRESS

BY NOW it should not surprise you to learn that people in the United States have grown dissatisfied with government.

At its modern peak in 1964, some 77 percent of those polled trusted the national government to do the right thing either always or most of the time; after decades in which that trust has eroded, by 2019, it was 17 percent (Pew Research Center 2019b). This decline in trust appears not just for government, however; over the past four decades or so people have expressed less faith in religious organizations, big business, newspapers, and banks, along with the U.S. Supreme Court, the presidency, and Congress (Gallup 2019). Confidence in Congress is especially low, with one poll showing its approval level lower than that for head lice, colonoscopies, root canals, cockroaches, and Genghis Khan (D. Matthews 2013; Public Policy Polling 2013). (It's worth noting that although people voice their displeasure with

Congress as an institution, they often express satisfaction with and support for their own members of Congress [Fenno 2003].)

More seriously, in a 2016 survey, 40 percent of respondents said that they had lost faith in democracy itself (Persily and Cohen 2016); by 2020, more than half of people in the United States "were dissatisfied with their system of government" (Foa et al. 2020). As we've seen, some of that dissatisfaction is rational. Yet there is a danger if this lack of trust causes people to withdraw even further from political and civic life. As I have emphasized, disengagement from the political system by those it does not serve well reduces the need for the system to respond to them, which leads to even weaker and less responsive policies, which can engender yet more disengagement and disgust. It's a potentially dangerous feedback loop.

To repeat: These feelings of disappointment, distrust, and despair are not unfounded. There's good and growing evidence that the national political system is unresponsive to the needs of all but the wealthiest among us (Achen and Bartels 2017; Bartels 2016; Bowman 2020; Erikson 2015; Gilens 2012; Gilens and Page 2014; Page and Gilens 2017), although this unresponsiveness is more pronounced among Republican than Democratic legislators (Brunner, Ross, and Washington 2013). Material conditions have gotten worse for most of us over the past decades—people really are working harder and harder with less to show for it (DeSilver 2018c; Schmitt, Gould, and Bivens 2018)—and some of this may be a reflection of the government's performance. More generally, in the words of one scholar, "Congress's problem-solving capacity appears to have fallen to new lows in recent years," and even unified one-party control does not guarantee that major legislative action will be possible (Binder 2015, 85).

And yet the 2018 election had the highest turnout for a midterm election in forty years and ushered in what was then the most diverse Congress in the history of the United States, even while democratic institutions and processes have arguably never been more dysfunctional or in greater peril (Azari 2019b). Of course, that turnout may not be a reflection of a healthy system but another reflection of dissatisfaction (we could think of the record high turnout in the 2020 presidential election in the same way), and the record diversity is largely a product of the changing demographics of the Democratic Party, not a broader pattern across the system.

While political scientists have struggled to find hard evidence for the influence of money on the political process (Baumgartner et al. 2009; Koerth 2019; Powell 2014), and some even make the argument that there is too *little* money in politics (Ansolabehere, de Figueiredo, and Snyder 2003), the conventional wisdom is that the U.S. political system is awash in money and the process is corrupted by it (Jones 2018). The old saying tells us that it's hard to get a person to understand something when their salary depends on their not understanding it. One careful review of research concludes that "although the empirical literature has not shown that money buys influence, there is evidence that the influx of money is correlated with the kinds of policy outputs that emerge from the legislative process" (Dawood 2015, 342), and there is good reason to believe that elected officials are responsive to the wishes of *donors*, if not the wealthy per se (Lee and McCarty 2019; McCarty 2019;

McKay 2018). This is yet another means by which dissatisfaction is fueled (and justified).

It's common for people to suggest that one solution to a dysfunctional and unrepresentative Congress that is too influenced by wealthy actors would be term limits. But political scientists are nearly unanimous in their opposition. As Seth Masket summarizes the consensus from research on the issue (which mostly examines state legislatures), "Term limits weaken legislatures (to the benefit of governors, parties, and lobbyists), increase polarization, and fail to achieve much of their good government goals" (Masket 2020). The principal problems with the U.S. policy-making system are structural ones, and you cannot fix a structural problem with personnel changes.

Similarly, no matter how much you think you do, you really don't want an outsider for the job. You will sometimes hear candidates make the case that what Washington, DC (or their state capitol or city hall) really needs is an outsider, a nonpolitician who can come in and shake things up and break down the old, failed ways of doing business—that all we need to do is to get everyone to sit down and set aside their partisan difference and make commonsense policies. There are a number of ways in which this is wrong, even if it might make intuitive sense. First, chief executive jobs, whether president, governor, or mayor, are complicated, demanding ones that require understanding of the workings of Byzantine systems, the motivations of other powerful actors and institutions, and something of the history of what's come before and why it succeeded or failed. Whether it's Jimmy Carter or Donald Trump, the record of those "outsiders" has not been good. Outsiders are likely to be incompetent.

Moreover, as noted previously, many (most?) of the problems we confront are structural ones; because the two parties are so thoroughly sorted by ideology, their disagreements are real ones—they have different policy goals and preferences. Sitting down for a beer and talking it over will not change the brute fact that they want different outcomes and that some of their constituencies care very deeply about those outcomes.

LESSONS FOR PRACTICE

To say that legislators are generally unresponsive to the needs of poor and low-income people is not to say that all legislators are unresponsive or that the legislature is never responsive. Legislators actually do care what you think; well, okay, they probably don't care what *you* think, but they do care what large, vocal groups of people care about (Jacobs and Shapiro 2000). Indeed, the odds that low-income people of color will be listened to are higher, evidence and history suggest, when they engage in mass protest (Gause 2020), as some have long argued (King 1963; Piven 2006; Piven and Cloward 1979)

If you find that an individual legislator opposes policies that would help your clients or your communities (or if they support policies that would harm them), then join with other organizations or individuals who are working to run against them (or run against them yourself). Meanwhile, make sure to let the elected officials whose work you respect and value know that—call, write, contribute, or share their good work on your social networks. There's more practical, how-to advice in the conclusion to this book, but for now bear in mind that it really does matter when people contact their legislators' offices: legislators keep track of who is calling on which issues, and if enough constituents express concern about a particular interest, it can absolutely shift lawmakers' focus and alter their behavior. Especially at the state and local level, remember that you may possess information they do not have that might change their behavior.

Chapter Fourteen

THE THING THEY SAY ABOUT
MAKING SAUSAGE IS TRUE

THERE'S ANOTHER old saying: If you like laws or sausages, it's best not to watch either being made. That's not bad advice. Lawmaking can be a grindingly slow, bloody, and chaotic process, and what emerges at the end of it—if anything emerges at all—may contain more gristle, hair, and snout than one might prefer.

One consequence of the increasing dysfunction of our national lawmaking institutions—caused in part by the policy drift you read about in chapter 10—is that the laws that do get enacted are suboptimal, relying on temporary fixes that can muster bare majority support, which often means that they are not the best solutions but merely the best ones available. These are what Steven Teles has referred to as legislative kludges, adopting the idea from computing, where a kludge is "an inelegant patch put in place to solve an unexpected problem and designed to be backward-compatible with the rest of an existing system." As he writes, "When you add up enough kludges, you get a very complicated program that has no clear organizing principle, is exceedingly difficult to understand, and is subject to crashes" (Teles 2013). That sounds a lot like the systems we have been trying to make sense of, doesn't it? Think of the forces pointed to in chapter 9 that shaped the design of the Affordable Care Act, for example. As kludges accumulate over time, policies become more irrational and less effective and engender greater decoherence (Drutman 2015; Wallach 2015); key components of the political and policy-making systems grow further apart, losing their connections to and communications with each other, creating chaos, confusion, and even more frustration with U.S. politics.

Whatever the system, achieving consensus among hundreds of people representing different regions with different problems and different interests is going to be difficult. But these ordinary challenges of lawmaking (often characterized by things that people might find distasteful, such as vote trading or inserting poison-pill amendments to intentionally reduce support for a bill) are heightened in a political system like ours that is so replete with veto points (see chapter 4). These opportunities for obstruction and delay are magnified within each house of Congress, where a single committee chair may be able to prevent a bill from getting a hearing or from being debated and voted on by the whole body. The House Rules Committee—"a tiny, airless closet deep in the labyrinth of the Capitol where some of the very meanest people on earth spend their days cleaning democracy like a fish," in the immortal words of Matt Taibbi (2005)—can then dictate how open the full debate is on a bill (how much time will be allotted to consideration of the issue and whether amendments will be permitted), for the few that get that far. And in the Senate, there's cloture (Rule 22), which requires a supermajority (three-fifths of senators) to agree to end debate and proceed to a vote; the mere threat of a filibuster can stop a bill from even being considered, an increasingly common tactic (Reynolds 2020).

This has consequences, of course. In the 116th Congress (2018–2020), more than sixteen thousand bills and resolutions were introduced in the House of Representatives; yet only 714 resolutions were passed (things like naming post offices or declaring, as they did that session, National Hydrogen and Fuel Cell Day or National Character Counts Week), and a scant 344 laws were enacted. In fact, of all the many thousands of bills introduced, only 746 of them even got as far as a full vote (GovTrack 2021). This figure is a bit deceptive: Because hyperpartisanship has made it even harder to get anything passed, Congress has taken to putting together things that might have once been separate bills on separate issues (especially during the annual budget process) into giant omnibus bills (DeSilver 2018a), so the total number of words that have been enacted into law has remained relatively constant at about four to six million per congressional session (GovTrack 2021). Nevertheless, this slow, acrimonious, minimally productive process may be yet another reason why so much of government, and Congress in particular, is not well loved.

LESSONS FOR PRACTICE

The legislative process is slow and frustrating at best, and often just plain incomprehensible, producing clumsy, kludgy results.

You probably don't need to study Senate procedure, but if you hope to have any influence on the process, you must know enough about it to intervene when it can make a difference. This is another instance in which focusing first on local politics often makes the most sense. Start going to open meetings of your school board or city council; most public bodies will post meeting schedules, agendas, and procedures online. Go to a few hearings and just listen, to build your knowledge about the formal process and who the important players are. Who chairs the key committees that deal with the issues that most concern you? Are there opportunities to learn about what they care about, or to meet them? Talk to other advocates and learn from them about what strategies they have found effective in the past. Building knowledge and influence takes time and some effort, but if you invest in it, you will radically increase your chances of affecting which issues get on the table and maybe even their outcomes. One of the benefits of what are often drawn-out processes is that they create multiple opportunities for you to weigh in and try to influence the outcome. And remember, it is never too late to start building your knowledge and getting more involved.

Chapter Fifteen

PRESIDENTS ARE WEAK AND COMMAND TOO MUCH OF OUR ATTENTION

PRESIDENTS ARE much less important than you think they are. This may seem a strange argument to make, given our experience of Donald Trump, but hear me out.

Because the president is the only official elected from across the entire nation, and because so much of the telling of U.S. history has been president-focused, we tend to pay enormous attention to what presidents do and to have outsize expectations of what they can achieve and the power they have to effect change. In extreme form, we slip into what political scientist Brandan Nyhan has called the Green Lantern theory of the presidency. If, like me, you were not much of a comic book reader, you may not know the Green Lantern. As I understand it, the extraordinary powers of the Green Lantern characters come from the rings they wear, which are fueled by their imaginations and their emotions; their power comes from sheer force of will. Too often we think that U.S. presidents, too, can do anything they like if they only try hard enough—if they give just the right speech or if they engage more persuasively and productively with members of Congress to change their minds or bring them together (E. Klein 2014; Nyhan 2009).

There's a much-beloved story among U.S. politics types about the inherent limits of presidential power. As historian Richard Neustadt tells it, President Truman sat in the Oval Office and contemplated General Dwight D. Eisenhower succeeding him as president: "He'll sit here, and he'll say Do this! Do that! *And nothing will happen.* Poor Ike—it won't be a bit like the army. He'll find it very frustrating" (Neustadt 1991, 10). There has been a consensus among political scientists that the U.S. presidency is an inherently weak office of limited powers, powers constrained by a host of forces beyond a president's reach. Examine Article II of the Constitution and you will find that the only power of the presidency that is not "checked"—that is, limited by another force within government—is the ability to grant pardons and reprieves. That's it.

But Daniel Drezner, a professor of international politics, argues that by the Trump era "the checks and balances constraining the presidency have worn thin" (Drezner 2020). Especially in matters of trade and foreign affairs, where Congress has ceded much authority to the chief executive and commander in chief of the armed forces, presidents have formal and informal powers that enable them to operate with broad discretion. Even in domestic affairs, thanks to executive orders and at least some putative control over the now massive federal bureaucracy— 2.1 million people work for the federal government (Jennings and Nagel 2019)—presidents have some ability to effect change on their own. And, as we have recently witnessed, many of the "guardrails" that limit executive power are not laws but norms—mere habit and custom—or regulations that turn out to be difficult or impossible to enforce. Witness the Trump administration's widespread disregard for congressional subpoenas and Congress's reluctance to turn to the courts for their enforcement. Or Trump's ability to hollow out the federal bureaucracy across multiple agencies to alter international trade and withdraw from international treaties, thereby weakening U.S. power and influence in the world. The implication of Drezner's book is that we must worry about such poorly constrained power in the hands of someone more competent to wield it than Donald Trump turned out to be.

And yet, as Trump himself would likely complain, those formal and informal constraints on the office can nonetheless radically alter presidents' ability to act as they see fit. The U.S. Supreme Court blocked Trump's efforts to add a question about citizenship status to the U.S. Census and to repeal the Obama-era Deferred Action for Childhood Arrivals (DACA) program; it stymied his efforts to restrict immigration to the United States from majority-Muslim countries (although it eventually acquiesced to a more narrowly tailored version of the policy); and federal and state courts alike thwarted his efforts to overturn the 2020 election (Shubber 2020). Other than the 2017 Tax Cuts and Jobs Act that disproportionately benefited high-income individuals and corporations, which any contemporary Republican-controlled Congress and Republican president would likely have enacted, and stacking the federal judiciary with right-wing ideologues thanks to the aggressive actions of Senate majority leader Mitch McConnell, there are few policy achievements that can be credited to the Trump administration. Even the Republican-controlled Senate obstructed him on funding the construction of a wall along the southern border, a payroll tax cut, withdrawal from the war in Afghanistan, and more.

Perhaps Trump was an especially enfeebled president because he never bothered to learn much about how things work and did not have the skills of negotiation and persuasion that effective governance requires, as Neustadt (1991) would have it, especially during our modern period of divided government, when different parties regularly control different branches. That's why, even when his party had unified control of government, so much of his time was devoted to issuing executive orders, many of them toothless, meaningless, or legally unsound, or launching screeds in 140-character bursts on Twitter. While he acted as if these directives or declarations were expressions of his power and strength, they were instead an indicator of his impotence, demonstrating his inability to achieve his preferred policies in a world of constrained authority. He didn't know how to govern, and apparently never tried to learn, so all that was left was bluster.

Drezner notes that this is "the paradox of a President who some political scientists view as autocratic and others view as spectacularly weak" (Drezner 2020, 181). We can perhaps see both his weakness and his strength in the fact that he was twice impeached by the U.S. House of Representatives (the equivalent of an indictment; he was only the third president in our history to be rebuked in this way even once) but seemed never to be in any serious danger of being convicted and removed from office by the Senate.

Political scientist Stephen Skowronek offers a different way for us to think about presidential power. We can understand something about a president's achievements and place in history, he says, by thinking about how one administration relates to those that preceded and followed. Using this approach, he suggests, there are four basic types of presidencies: reconstructive, articulative, disjunctive, and preemptive.

Reconstructive presidents—Jefferson, Jackson, Lincoln, FDR, and Reagan—are distinct not chiefly because of their skills or the way they employ the resources available to them but because of *when* they try to achieve what they try to achieve. They come to power when the previous regime is in disrepute or disarray and stand in opposition to that regime and what it stood for. Thus, they come into office "beyond all semblance of political order." Franklin Delano Roosevelt is the prototypical reconstructive president: Because he campaigned and sought to govern in staunch opposition to Hoover's disastrous response to the Great Depression, he had an unusual opportunity to make transformational change, and he took advantage of that opportunity. Articulative presidents come to power in express affiliation with a prior regime that is "resilient"—that is, it still has strength and legitimacy; Monroe, Polk, Teddy Roosevelt, and Lyndon Johnson fit in here. Because their mandate is to further someone else's goals, not their own, they do not have the opportunity for the kind of transformation available to reconstructive presidents (think of LBJ as trying to complete the unfinished work of the New Deal). Preemptive presidents— Tyler, Andrew Johnson, Wilson, and Nixon—come to power in opposition to a strong regime; their chief hindrance is that they are struggling against the institutionalized power and support of their ideological opponents. Finally, there are the disjunctive presidents—John Quincy Adams, Pierce, Hoover, Carter—who come to power affiliated with a weak regime. They are in a bind, for they cannot repudiate a regime as a reconstructive president can, nor can they too strenuously support or benefit from their weak one. As a result, these are the presidents who most consistently find themselves identified as the worst at the job (Skowronek 1997).

Julia Azari, a former student of Skowronek, wrestled with which type of president Donald Trump was and concluded that, though a complicated case, he was ultimately disjunctive, having been unable to reconcile the needs of the nation with the demands of the party and his own coalition within it (Azari 2019a). Perhaps his inability to provide what the nation most needed in 2020—an effective national strategy to control the coronavirus pandemic—and his electoral defeat make this easier to see and also make it easier to see the limited nature of his achievements in office.

LESSONS FOR PRACTICE

While political scientists have found lots to engage and argue with in this formulation, here's why I think it's useful: When thinking about how much power a president (or any leader) has to effect change, we need to think beyond the formal powers of the office or the management skills of the officeholder and think about the context in which that leader operates. Is there a new executive director (ED) coming into your agency? What's the reputation of the old regime led by the former ED (are you all happy or disappointed to see that person go)? Is the new ED seeking to continue on the previous course or proposing large-scale change? Will that be welcomed or disruptive? Thinking through the context can help you think about how effective the new ED is likely to be and then how to more effectively help or hinder, depending on what you think is best for the organization and those it serves.

On the macro level, try to pay less attention to the president. That's hard, especially if the president is someone like Donald Trump, but you will have a better understanding of what's really going on if you attend more to Congress, the courts, and what's happening in your own state legislature and city government.

Chapter Sixteen

IT REALLY IS THE ECONOMY, STUPID

JUST AS we attend too much to the president and the presidency and therefore risk missing other sources of power and opportunities for policy change, so too do we pay too much attention to election campaigns and the quadrennial presidential election. While political scientists disagree on precisely how, when, and why traditional campaign activity matters, there is consensus that it likely matters around the margins at best and is less important than other factors in trying to make sense of who wins and loses these contests. It's one of the lessons to be drawn from a list of "rules" that hung inside Bill Clinton's first campaign headquarters as the country was mired in recession:

Change vs. more of the same
The economy, stupid
Don't forget health care.

In a general election, party affiliation will determine how most people vote: most Democrats will vote for the Democrat and most Republicans will vote for the Republican. Other voters enter the voting booth with an assessment of how things are going economically and how well they themselves are doing: if they conclude that things are going well, they vote for the incumbent; if they judge things to be going poorly, they vote for the challenger. These judgments are typically made, by the way, independent of whether the incumbent administration can logically be held responsible for those outcomes. One infamous study (probably wrong, alas) claimed that New Jersey voters punished Woodrow Wilson at the voting booth for a series of local shark attacks (Achen and Bartels 2017; Anson and Hellwig 2015; Bartels 2014; Fowler and Hall 2018; Linn, Nagler, and Morales 2010).

There is not good evidence that all of the things we tend to focus on during general elections campaigns—television and radio ads, door-to-door canvassing, fliers, debates—have much impact. These things can matter for primary campaigns, when each party is choosing someone to go up against the other party's candidate, but when a Democrat is battling a Republican in the general election, voters are so attached to their own party that all of that (often very expensive) campaign activity is, with rare exceptions, not going to change minds or votes. There are, however, some important caveats. Campaigns can and do alter voter turnout; media coverage of campaigns and the issues that gain prominence (and how they are framed) may affect some voters' decision making; television advertising may have a greater impact on "down-ballot" races (for governor, U.S.

House member, and U.S. senator, for example) than they do on presidential contests; and "deep canvassing," involving lengthy, nonjudgmental, personal interactions with voters, may well have persuasive effects (D. P. Green, McGrath, and Aronow 2013; Kalla and Broockman 2018, 2020; Sides and Vavreck 2013; Groenendyk and Krupnikov 2020; Woodly 2018; Sides, Vavreck, and Warshaw 2020).

This is another effect of hyperpartisanship in the contemporary period, of course, and more reason to accept the uncomfortable truth that, in most cases, attempts at persuasion may be futile or so difficult as to be economically inefficient (see chapter 21). But this may be less troubling than it appears. Now that the two U.S. political parties have been so effectively "sorted" (see chapter 7), most voters' decisions will not be appreciably altered by learning the policy positions of the candidates because those positions are likely to align closely with their party. Thus, knowing nothing but whether a candidate is a Democrat or a Republican is an effective shorthand that allows voters to reliably support the candidate most in sync with their views. In a world of information overload, maybe that's not all bad.

LESSONS FOR PRACTICE

Note the qualifications made about the claims in this chapter. The ordinary activity of two well-funded campaigns during a national contest for the presidency likely has minimal effect in changing people's minds. But those same activities during those same campaigns can increase the number of people who show up to vote, and those activities in primary contests and in state and local ones can have much greater effects. This is another instance in which paying less attention to national politics and more attention to what is taking place closer to home can be a better use of your time, money, and energies. There are elections happening where you live every year, sometimes multiple times in a year. Make a commitment to know about those local offices and the contests to fill them. Learn about the candidates, find the ones who best represent your policy preferences and those of the people and populations you care about, and then reach out to them to find out how you can help. You may be surprised by how warmly you are welcomed and how deeply you can be engaged if you want to be. Remember: Democracy is a practice.

Chapter Seventeen

JUDGES ARE PLAYERS, NOT UMPIRES

DURING THE Senate hearings that would ultimately confirm his nomination to be chief justice of the United States Supreme Court, John G. Roberts said this: "Judges and Justices are servants of the law, not the other way around. Judges are like umpires. Umpires don't make the rules, they apply them" (J. Roberts 2005). Roberts may have believed this, but that does not make the claim any less absurd. Start with his analogy. Although we might expect that Major League Baseball umpires, at the top of their profession, would almost always identify whether a pitch was a ball or a strike and that any two umpires would make the same calls, we would be wrong. Careful analysis by Boston University scholars showed that umpires made the objectively wrong call some 20 percent of the time (Williams 2019).

Then there's the premise that there are clearly laid out rules and that a judge's job is merely to apply them to the facts of the case before them. Yet it is common for Supreme Court justices (and judges on other appeals courts) to come to widely differing conclusions. Just in the 2019–2020 term, the Supreme Court issued thirteen rulings with a 5–4 or 5–3 split (five justices said the law or the Constitution demanded one remedy while three or four said that the law or the Constitution demanded another), which is 20 percent of all their decisions (coincidentally, about the same "error rate" as baseball umpires). Moreover, more than 70 percent of that term's decisions overruled the decision of a lower federal court, which is also generally staffed by accomplished jurists (Ballotpedia 2020c). From 2000 to 2018, more than a third of all Supreme Court decisions were unanimous (showing perhaps that there are particular areas of the law or kinds of cases in which biases are not activated or less evident), but just under 20 percent were 5–4 splits (Turberville and Marcum 2018). If it is such a straightforward matter to apply the law in a neutral fashion, then why do judges disagree so often?

It is disingenuous to pretend that judges—including Supreme Court justices—are not as much political actors as are members of Congress or the president or to pretend, especially when we are talking about interpreting the Constitution, that the "rules" are clear and obvious. Take the very first words of the First Amendment: "Congress shall make no law respecting the establishment of religion, or prohibiting the free exercise thereof." Right off the bat, the Constitution is articulating two principles that are in tension with each other; in any particular instance, the task before the judge is to decide how to balance these two conflicting values. Where they draw that line—how they achieve that balance—is a matter of, well, *judgment*, and is inescapably rooted in their own worldview and their ways of thinking about the law (including which previous decisions are most relevant and most important), the appropriate limits on state power, how encompassing individual freedom can and should be, and so on. Their biases will frame how they approach the question, and there is no human being without bias if we understand that word to mean "ways of seeing and making sense of the world."

We all know this at some level. Why was there such tumult over the 2020 death of Justice Ruth Bader Ginsberg and President Trump's nomination of Amy Coney Barrett? Because Ginsberg's policy preferences and manner of interpreting the law were well known and Barrett's previous writings made her politics clear as well. Barrett was nominated not despite her revealed or presumed political preferences but because of them; presidents choose one accomplished jurist over another in hopes that their choice will implement their policy goals better than others would. People who insist that there is neutral judicial decision making are lying to themselves, to you, or both. The Supreme Court is not merely a legal branch but a political one too; once we recognize this, the rest makes more sense.

I wrote in chapter 1 about the inherently undemocratic structure of the U.S. Supreme Court. Its members are nominated by an official who rises to office thanks to an undemocratic Electoral College; they are then confirmed by an undemocratic Senate to what are, in practice, lifetime appointments. (The Constitution provides that justices shall serve "during good behavior" and that their salaries may never be reduced; in our entire history, only one justice, Samuel Chase, was impeached by the House, but he was not convicted and removed by the

Senate.) Once in office, they are virtually unaccountable to the public. There is literally no other democracy whose highest court does not have term limits or a mandatory retirement age (or both) (Calabresi and Lindgren 2006), and the only U.S. state with lifetime appointments is Rhode Island (Golde 2020).

On one level, there is a virtue in lifetime appointment. It insulates federal judges from the passions of the public, allows them to rule without concern for securing or maintaining popularity, and protects them from pressures from Congress and the executive. Most political scientists oppose electing judges of any kind, even though all but seven states do so (Ballotpedia 2020b), because it creates a range of perverse incentives and opportunities for corruption and undue influence. In this way of thinking, the antidemocratic nature of our federal courts is a positive feature of the system.

At the same time, there remains the "countermajoritarian difficulty" of the institution (Bickel 1986). Imagine this scenario: All members of the House of Representatives vote in favor of a wildly popular new law to respond to a national emergency; every member of the Senate—Republican, Democrat, and Independent— also then votes for that same law, which the president then eagerly signs. In the face of that overwhelming democratic responsiveness to the wants and needs of the public, as few as five people, if they happened to be Supreme Court justices, could invalidate that law and render the popular will utterly meaningless.

It's not as if this is something of this kind has not happened. The most notorious example may be from the Great Depression era. Franklin Delano Roosevelt was elected after a campaign that promised public works projects, cash relief, unemployment insurance, old age pensions, and more (Rauchway 2018). Once he took office, with new laws enacted by large congressional majorities, he and his team began to implement a broad array of such programs to bring help to a desperate public and to try to salvage an economy in collapse; these are the initiatives we now associate with the New Deal. But throughout the early to mid-1930s, an exceedingly conservative Supreme Court struck down many of those laws, claiming (credibly, truth be told) that they exceeded the powers granted to the federal government under the Constitution. Only when Roosevelt threatened to "pack the court"—that is, to have Congress pass a law that would create more seats on the Court and then appoint new justices sympathetic to the New Deal agenda—did the court back down and allow the federal government to address the crisis largely as it saw fit. You might hear this referred to as the "switch in time that saved nine" (Ho and Quinn 2010).

Part of what has given the Supreme Court whatever legitimacy it may have is that it often affirms public sentiment, especially on contentious social issues, rather than challenging it. The rights of women to access abortion services and of same-sex couples to marry are positions supported by large majorities of the public (Pew Research Center 2019c, 2019d), and the Court has generally followed public opinion rather than leading it (Casillas, Enns, and Wohlfarth 2011). But if a radically anti-majoritarian post-Ginsberg Court seeks to abolish or radically limit these or other rights, the Court may find its popularity falling closer to the level of Congress's (see chapter 13).

This popular trust matters. While Congress has the budget, the authority, and the resources to enforce its will even if it has little public support, the Supreme Court does not. In this way, it is an inherently weak branch. Here's how Alexander Hamilton put in in *Federalist* no. 78 (Hamilton, Madison, and Jay [1788] 1992):

> Whoever attentively considers the different departments of power must perceive, that, in a government in which they are separated from each other, the judiciary, from the nature of its functions, will always be the least dangerous to the political rights of the Constitution; because it will be least in a capacity to annoy or injure them. The Executive not only dispenses the honors, but holds the sword of the community. The legislature not only commands the purse, but prescribes the rules by which the duties and rights of every citizen are to be regulated. The judiciary, on the contrary, has no influence over either the sword or the purse; no direction either of the strength or of the wealth of the society; and can take no active resolution whatever. It may truly be said to have neither FORCE nor WILL, but merely judgment; and must ultimately depend upon the aid of the executive arm even for the efficacy of its judgments.

If the only power the Supreme Court has to enforce its decisions is our collective willingness to abide by them, it's a very unstable source of strength indeed.

But what gives courts the power to strike down laws in the first place? Where does this power of judicial review come from? Not the Constitution. Article III, which creates federal courts, is among the shortest, and while Sections 1 and 2 talk of the "judicial power," they don't actually say what that is. But in an 1803 case, *Marbury v. Madison*, the Court asserted that it had the right to determine whether a law comported with the provisions of the Constitution, and if it determined that it did not, then the Court could nullify it. It's an extraordinary power for a court to assert for itself.

But why do we abide by it? Well, we don't always. President Andrew Jackson supposedly said, in response to a decision about tribal lands that he did not care for: "[Chief Justice] John Marshall has made his decision; now let him enforce it!" And, of course, there is the 1954 case of *Brown v. Board of Education of Topeka*, in which the Court's edict to desegregate public schools was met with a program of massive resistance throughout the South; as a practical matter, given the continued segregation of U.S. schools by race even to this day (Garcia 2020; Reardon and Owens 2014), *Brown* has arguably never been implemented (even after Title IV of the Civil Rights Act of 1964 gave the executive expanded enforcement powers).

This points to one way to deal with antimajoritarian courts (which may grow even more reactionary and repressive given the current conservative majority): we could simply ignore them. This suggestion was made by policy analyst Matt Bruenig in the wake of Justice Ginsberg's death: Reject *Marbury v. Madison* as wrongly decided, he suggests, and take the Court's opinions as merely advisory (Bruenig 2020). If Hamilton was correct about their weakness, what are they going to do?

Perhaps less radical would be to look for ways to depoliticize the court and to limit its influence. We could expand its size (and that of the lower federal courts, which are understaffed and overburdened) and impose term limits on all federal judges, something students of the courts from across the political spectrum have been recommending for many years (Golde 2020). This would create regular turnover on the court, minimize the influence of any single justice or set of presidential appointments (and simultaneously ratchet down the stakes of any single nomination), reduce the current incentives to appoint very young judges to maximize their tenure and impact, and grant each administration equal opportunity to imprint its political preferences on the federal courts. Congress can also enact laws that limit the Court's jurisdiction, as it has in the past (Peck 2018), or require a supermajority for the Court's decisions to have legal force to alter the balance of power in the federal government.

LESSONS FOR PRACTICE

We take a lot for granted and can fall into the trap of assuming that just because something has been done a certain way for an extended period of time it must always be done in that way. But it need not be so. U.S. courts are antimajoritarian and antidemocratic, and we can work to change that by recognizing that Congress has the constitutional power to alter them so that they have less power and better represent the nation's diversity. Don't ever assume that because a court has made a ruling it is necessarily fair or just or even well-reasoned; judges have enormous power, and we must assume that, like anyone with power, they will use it. Demystifying these institutions is a first step toward turning them toward more democratic ends. They must earn trust and respect, not simply command it.

Chapter Eighteen

PEOPLE AREN'T DUMB BUT THEY SURE ARE IGNORANT

MOST PEOPLE in the United States do not possess deep, substantive knowledge of politics and policy making. Many do not even have a good command of basic facts. One recent survey by the Annenberg Public Policy Center revealed that only 39 percent of respondents could name all three branches of government and that 22 percent could not name even one. This was actually an improvement over prior years. In other surveys, more than 60 percent could not name the party that had majority control of the House or the Senate at the time, about half knew that the vice president's vote breaks a tie in the Senate, and just four in ten knew how many votes are needed to end a Senate filibuster (sixty) (Annenberg Public Policy Center 2014, 2019; Pew Research Center 2018a). People often estimate that foreign aid is 25 percent or more of the federal budget (it's less than 1 percent; the largest expenditures are for the military, Medicare, Medicaid, and Social Security) (DiJulio, Firth, and Brodie 2015;

Williamson 2019), and for decades now, as crime rates have been declining (even considering a rise in shootings and homicides in 2020), most still think that crime is and has been on the rise (Koerth and Thomson-DeVeaux 2020). Perhaps even more troubling, people are unsure about their state's rules and procedures governing how, when, and whether they can vote—this is true even among voters with higher levels of education (Vandermaas-Peeler et al. 2018)—and fully 60 percent cannot say which party controls their state senate or state house of representatives (Hertel-Fernandez and Guillermo Smith 2020).

There is an important caveat: When we ask people about the political institutions that are most directly implicated in their own lives, they sometimes demonstrate deep knowledge. AFDC recipients, for example, could display significant knowledge of how those relief systems functioned (Soss 1999), and people who live in highly policed communities often have extensive knowledge of those institutions and how they operate; as a result, they form not only attitudes about government but also strategies for avoiding engagement with its agents (Weaver, Prowse, and Piston 2019). Thus, when we claim that people are ignorant about politics and policy, that is true if we are talking about the policies that are abstract to them and distant from their lives. People may not know how many justices there are on the Supreme Court or the name of the secretary of defense, but they may very well know what the asset limit is for those seeking SNAP benefits or which public housing developments near them are the best (or worst) maintained.

That said, the general point holds: There is widespread ignorance about many issues of politics and policy. This is not a new development, despite the tendency of some people to insist that recent generations are less informed than previous ones ("kids these days!"). Overall political knowledge has fluctuated little since the mid-1900s. People today may not know enough about politics and the workings of U.S. political systems, but they never really have (Delli Carpini and Keeter 1996). As political scientists have noted for more than half a century, most people do not have a coherent, consistent set of political beliefs, and the beliefs that they do hold are tenuous (Converse 1964).

To take an example: Many Republicans were accused of being hypocritical for shifting their position on free trade after Donald Trump became president and pursued new tariffs and protectionist policies, but this is a fairly predictable (and common) occurrence. One cleverly designed experiment showed that many Republicans (especially less knowledgeable ones) are party loyalists rather than true conservatives in any meaningful sense; their support or opposition to ten different policies could be altered by whether they were told President Trump supported or opposed them (Barber and Pope 2019). And while greater levels of factual knowledge about politics can sometimes help prevent people from believing false statements or propaganda, highly engaged conservatives with more political knowledge are even *more* likely to believe baseless conspiracy theories that are consistent with their worldview (Miller, Saunders, and Farhart 2016). If you expect people to be consistent and coherent in their political positions, you will be disappointed. Most people are not rational in the way we might like to think.

This ignorance of policy, politics, and procedures makes sense at some level: U.S. politics is complicated, as this book argues at length, and most people simply don't have the time or the interest to develop a richer understanding of the issues and players involved. As a result, their political socialization derives not from careful thought but from what they absorb from their associations with family, friends, community and religious organizations, media, or political parties that provide them with cues about which positions to take. It may be that we are less informed and less engaged than citizens of other countries (Torney-Purta and Barber 2004; DeSilver 2018b) because we, on average, work more hours for worse outcomes, leaving less time and less mental and emotional energy available for effecting political change. Of course, that withdrawal from politics (and the concomitant distrust of the system) exacerbates the problem, making policies even less responsive to their needs and their lives and making them less able to foster their own education, action and activism. Thus, there is a genuine threat to democracy if the citizenry is not well informed: How will people act in their own interests?

But it's not clear that people even want to be more involved or informed; they might prefer what John Hibbing and Elizabeth Theiss-Morse called "stealth democracy." People would like for there to be democratic outcomes, but they don't necessarily need to be a part of them or want to see those processes in action; in many instances, they would just as soon have independent experts make key decisions, especially if that would make politics less confrontational (Hibbing and Theiss-Morse 2002; VanderMolen 2017). This finding—that people don't like confrontation—is especially troubling to those of us who believe that politics is inescapably confrontational:

Take away the confrontation, the disagreements, and the disputes, and you are taking away diversity of opinion, perspective, and preferences. If people are not arguing, then someone is probably not being heard. All of this is further complicated by the fact that people generally underestimate the extent to which others disagree with them; they may believe that confrontation is unnecessary in part because they misunderstand how much actual distance there is between groups on various issues (Hibbing and Theiss-Morse 2002).

LESSONS FOR PRACTICE

We might think of this as good news: Instead of social workers having to persuade large numbers of their compatriots of the virtues or value of one policy or another, they can work to persuade party leaders (whether local, state, or national) to shift their position or to advocate more actively for or against it. This is another reason to be engaged in local politics, because your ability to alter the party position could have a significant impact and might be easier to accomplish than trying to persuade large numbers of people. Because most people are party loyalists rather than policy loyalists (Barber and Pope 2019), a new message from a few leaders at the top could have far-reaching effects. But it's also important never to assume that people know about the issues you are talking about; you will likely need to make your case over and over and over again for it to be heard and understood.

Chapter Nineteen

THERE IS NO PUBLIC

JUST BECAUSE people are uninformed does not mean that they do not have opinions about politics and policy, and many will even answer a pollster's questions about a topic they know nothing about. This is not surprising, perhaps, when you consider that few people want to appear to be out of touch. Thus, a poll's reported findings about public preferences on some issue may include responses from people who never had a position on it until the moment they formed one when responding to the poll. As one eminent scholar of this so-called public opinion put it:

> Most people really aren't sure what their opinions are on most political matters, including even such completely personal matters as their level of interest in politics. They're not sure because there are few occasions, outside of a standard interview situation, in which they are called upon to formulate and express political opinions. So, when confronted by

rapid-fire questions in a public opinion survey, they make up attitude reports as best they can as they go along. But because they are hurrying, they are heavily influenced by whatever ideas happen to be at the top of their minds. (Zaller 1992, 76)

People also lie to pollsters. They lie about their voting behavior (more people regularly report having voted than actual did so, for example). They lie about matters they think of as private, such as their income or their sexual behavior. And they lie about anything that they worry might reflect badly upon them, such as their eating or exercise habits, the frequency of their church attendance, their drug and alcohol consumption, and so on (Prosser and Mellon 2018; Lax, Phillips, and Stollwerk 2016).

Polling is also notoriously sensitive to how questions are worded. Ask people about "welfare," and majorities will be opposed to spending more money; but ask about "assistance to poor people," and majorities will support increasing aid (Howard et al. 2017; Gilens 1999).

Finally, there remains a host of methodological challenges even among diligent pollsters, especially in a world of declining response rates (fewer and fewer people will answer a call from an unknown number). For our purposes, it's especially important to note the likelihood of missing people without internet access or phones (since that is how most polls are now conducted); those people tend to be disproportionately poor and in unstable housing conditions.

As a result, your best bet is to ignore most polls. As we've discussed (see chapter 18), most people are inattentive and poorly informed, and polls are not typically good gauges of deeply held or well-informed beliefs; they are often at best a reflection of which media story (or position) has been dominant lately and has therefore primed people to be thinking about a particular issue or, because of framing effects, to think about it in a particular way.

You should likewise be suspicious if a politician tells you that "what the people want" is one thing or another, or that "the American people believe" something in particular. In a nation of some 330 million, all kinds of people believe all sorts of things—or say they do. But there is no such thing as "the people"; at best there are many peoples, and to generalize about what they want is a perilous affair. This is what I mean when I assert that there is no public.

Opinion may matter less than you think, anyway. As chapters 1 and 13 show, national politicians are generally unresponsive to the desires of the majority, and despite the conventional wisdom, they don't adjust their policy positions or voting behavior in response to opinion as it is revealed in polls; they are much more likely to adopt a position and then work to persuade voters that it's the right one. That is to say that, as a rule, "politicians don't pander" (Jacobs and Shapiro 2000).

LESSONS FOR PRACTICE

All that having been said, there is such a thing as good, reliable polling; you will see throughout this book that I have often drawn upon the work of Pew Research Center, for example, which strives to undertake sound work. How can you tell? Start by looking for transparency. Can you find a detailed description of the poll's methodology? Are you told which people were polled, and how many? When was the poll conducted? By what method? Is the polling instrument (the questions asked) available in its entirely? Are the questions clear? Does the polling outfit reveal its funding sources and any potential conflicts of interest? Is the polling organization careful not to overstate its findings and to put them into useful context to help readers consider their meaning? (American Association for Public Opinion Research 2020; Sotomayor 2020).

Polling has its uses, but we must be careful about the conclusions we draw from even sound, sophisticated polling operations—and we should never conclude anything at all from a single poll. Instead, look for patterns and trends over time or for websites that are aggregators of poll results from multiple polls conducted by multiple polling firms to show trends over time (see fivethirtyeight.com for an example).

Finally, be wary of anyone asserting that something must be done (or cannot be done) because "the people" support it (or do not support it). Always ask, "which people?" And "how do we know this?"

Chapter Twenty

THERE IS NO VIEW FROM NOWHERE

PART OF why people in the United States tend to be ill-informed about substantive matters of politics and policy is that there is no easy way for them to acquire useful, relevant knowledge. In a better functioning democracy, this is a role that media would perform. Alexis de Tocqueville, a French aristocrat who wrote about us when we were a new nation, said that media (he referred then only to newspapers) were an essential component of democracy because they were the only means by which disparate citizens could readily learn about the important issues of the day to make informed decisions about their governance; he went even further, arguing that "to suppose that [newspapers] only serve to protect freedom would be to diminish their importance: they maintain civilization" (Tocqueville [1835–1840] 2004, book 2, chap. 6).

But despite their abundance (or maybe because of it?), political media today do not generally make it easy for people to acquire useful knowledge that will make them better citizens. In part the problem is that political journalists misunderstand their role and think that their job is to be "objective" and tell "both sides" of a story rather than to serve as a check on government itself and help people make sense of complicated matters. I put "objective" in quotes precisely because there is no such thing as objectivity. We are all biased, each in our own way, as I noted in chapter 17, if we recognize that bias is nothing more than our way of seeing the world and making sense of it. There is no view from nowhere—no utterly neutral vantage point from which we can describe the political world (Nagel 1989; Rosen 2010). As one political scientist put it, "Facts don't exist independent of interpretive lenses" (Stone 2012). Or, in the words of a famous community organizer, "All of life is partisan. There is no dispassionate objectivity" (Alinsky 1971).

While no one is unbiased, and journalists, like judges, should not pretend that they have some special status in this regard, they can instead aspire to intellectual honesty: revealing their own ways of thinking and showing the reader how they have come to their particular understanding of the day's events. The mission of political media in a democratic polity should not be to tell every side of a story with equal weight and leave it to the reader to sort it out, but to tell the truth as they see it, to help inattentive and generally inexpert readers or viewers make sense of complicated political and policy issues, and to point out when they are being lied to, exploited, or told half-truths. What people need is *context* that will help them make sense of particular events: Is what politicians are saying consistent with what they have said before or with their actions? Has this policy approach been tried in the past? What happened? Are there interest groups behind the scenes pushing for a particular outcome? Who benefits from what's being proposed? Are the arguments that are being made rooted in reliable evidence and sound data? Absent this information—which requires that journalists have deep knowledge and informed understanding of the issues they cover—it's hard for most observers to know what to make of current events. Moreover, pretending not to have viewpoints and agendas obscures for viewers the potential economic and class biases of many media organizations, which are often mere profit centers for multinational corporate conglomerates (Herman and Chomsky 2002; Lichter 2017).

Big newspapers will occasionally do a context story (a "deep dive"), but you can't do this just once, because most people know too little and don't pay consistent attention. When journalists do talk about policy, they too often get stuck in shallow "gotcha" games because too many don't have policy knowledge and are stretched too thin because of the decimation of the newspaper industry. Health policy is a good example. During the 2020 Democratic primary debates, the only question moderators seemed to want to ask about various plans to expand access to health insurance or medical care was "How will you pay for it?" If you know anything about the operations of U.S. health policy, then you know that we already spend more money per person than any other rich democracy and yet have among the worst health outcomes and lowest rates of access to care, so you know how unhelpful a question that is.

Media are at their worst during presidential election years. They spend more time offering guesses about how people will vote than helping people make good decisions about how to vote.

This long-standing challenge is even harder today. Social media shifted us from a one-to-many form of communication, epitomized by a TV broadcast or newspaper that pushes its coverage out to many people, to a many-to-many world, in which each of us, thanks to a range of new media platforms, can share news, perspectives, research, or calls for mobilization with large numbers of others (Gillmor 2006)—very large numbers of others if one of your posts goes viral and is circulated by someone with a mammoth audience. While the overall leading source of political news remains television, nearly 20 percent of people in the United States get their political news primarily through one social media platform or another. These people tend to be younger, generally inattentive, and less engaged; they are less informed than any other group except for those who get most of their news from local television. They are also, by the way, the most likely to have encountered unfounded conspiracy theories (Mitchell et al. 2020).

Democrats and Republicans increasingly live in different media universes, with Republicans reliant overwhelmingly on Fox News and Democrats drawing much more broadly from CNN, NBC, ABC, and MSNBC. That said, there is no single media source that more than half of us trust (Jurkowitz et al. 2020). But this dominance of Fox among Republicans creates what scholars refer to as epistemic closure—a closed media ecosystem, or news bubble, in which outside information that challenges the party narrative is excluded. Although objectivity does not exist, propaganda absolutely does. There is good evidence that watching Fox News actually *reduces* people's substantive political knowledge (Cassino, Wooley, and Jenkins 2012; Cassino and Wooley 2011; Licari 2020). Fox and other (disproportionately right-wing) advocacy media might be more properly thought of as propaganda outlets rather than news organizations (Illing 2019; Democracy Forward 2020; Yglesias 2018; Holt 2019). The rise of Newsmax and One America Network as sources for those who worry that Fox has become too liberal (or insufficiently pro-Trump) makes this trend even more worrisome if it results in large numbers of people being even more disconnected from anything we would recognize as shared reality (Illing 2020).

In sum, news media in the United States have failed to fulfill their function as de Tocqueville understood it, and that continued failure is part of how we explain our enfeebled democracy.

LESSONS FOR PRACTICE

Do not watch television news. With exceedingly rare exceptions, it will not deliver helpful, informed coverage of policy and politics. Think of your TV only as a place for entertainment. Instead, read broadly and read critically, getting to know the sources that consistently cover the issues and populations you care about, and look for ways to get relevant information pushed to you on a regular basis—email lists, newsletters, Twitter (if you carefully curate your Follow list, it can be a tremendous resource), or local neighborhood listservs. When in doubt, or when it's important to you to really understanding something, compare how multiple outlets cover the story or issue you care about. This triangulation technique will help you develop what may be the most important habit of news consumption: Never depend on a single source for information about anything. As you build your own habits of responsibly informed citizenship, help other people also find better sources of information and analysis. Get in the habit of checking out sites like the *Columbia Journalism Review* (cjr.org), Poynter.org and Snopes.com for critical coverage of media.

Meanwhile, turn off Facebook to the extent you can, or at least find ways to productively intervene in your social media networks when misinformation is being spread. Remember the truth sandwich: If you are trying to correct false information or outright propaganda, be careful not to elevate the falsehood or spread it further; instead, state clearly what we know to be true, identify the false or misleading claim and how we know it's false, and conclude by restating the truth. The headline, if there is one, should be the true claim, not the false one; that just further circulates the falsehood. Sharing information from attentive fact-checkers like Snopes.com can't hurt, but it's unclear how much it will help.

While you're at it, find ways to support local media, which are in crisis as more and more local papers are being shut down for lack of resources or bought out by national conglomerates without any connection to or concern for the local community (Hendrickson 2019; Sullivan 2020; Grieco 2020). What's going on in school board or zoning commission meetings may have a greater direct impact on your life in the short term than the debates in Congress that make for national news, and without good local reporting few people will have any way of knowing what decisions are being made and by whom. This is yet another space where, as I've noted, you have a greater chance of affecting outcomes: find local journalism, and find ways to support it. The *New York Times* hosts a useful tool that will help you locate outlets near you: nytimes.com/interactive/2020/us/support-local -journalism.html.

Chapter Twenty-One

YOU WILL NOT CHANGE ANYONE'S MIND

PEOPLE ARE irrational. You probably know this from your practice or from your family. They are not *always* irrational, of
course, and not about all things, but people will often act out of
instinct, emotion, or habit, even in ways that are not in their best
interest (Ariely 2009). But too often when we consider people
as political actors (and especially when they are thought of as
economic actors), there can be a presumption—often unspoken
and even unacknowledged—that people are engaged in rational
decision making. This presumption suggests that when people
are deciding how to vote, they identify the policy positions of
each candidate, evaluate them according to how well they cor-
respond to the voter's own preferences, values, or concerns, and
then choose the candidate who is the best match.

But people don't behave in this way in virtually any aspect
of their lives, including voting or adopting policy positions.
And as we have seen, even if people did try to engage in such a

deliberative process, they do not typically possess the substantive knowledge that would enable them to do so. How, then, do people make decisions about voting? They look for cues, or cognitive shortcuts, that enable them to engage in a kind of bounded rationality—what economist Herbert Simon called "satisficing" (Simon 1997). Political parties, as we have seen, serve as one important source of cues for people; instead of evaluating each candidate or issue one by one, we can look at which candidates and policies our party endorses. This method may not always give us 100 percent satisfaction, but it is much more efficient than the alternative and gives us results that are good enough. That's the idea of *satisficing*—and it is a useful way to understand how most people come to their politics.

Sometimes our thinking is even less rational. By the time we are adults, we have constructed a robust set of positions and beliefs. When thinking about the political world, we begin with those beliefs, those inherent biases, and then work backward (often unconsciously) to fit whatever facts we are being presented with into that preexisting schema. Our minds use this motivated reasoning to protect us from cognitive dissonance—information that could unsettle our established beliefs or worldview. As a consequence, our brains literally process information differently depending on whether it fits with or challenges a preexisting belief; we call this phenomenon "confirmation bias" (Kaplan, Gimbel, and Harris 2016). This helps explain why presenting people with evidence showing that they are incorrect about something can make them *less* likely to change their minds—they double down on their position, adopting a defensive crouch (Hoffman 2019). And even when new information succeeds in altering people's political or policy opinions, those effects tend to be short-lived, and people eventually revert back to their original stance (even though they may retain the new factual information!) (Dowling, Henderson, and Miller 2020).

You might think that people with more education would be more open to alternate political viewpoints and more willing to alter their stance, but that is not the case (Ganzach and Schul 2020), and new research suggests that politicians in particular are less open to persuasion and more resistant to information that challenges their biases (Christensen and Moynihan 2020). This is why you might be wise not to devote too much time and energy to trying to change the mind of a U.S. senator if you see that they are committed to a position; you're likely better off working to replace them with someone who already agrees with you. By the time someone has attained that office, they tend to have a well-established set of views and, for a host of reasons, be reluctant to alter them. Persuasion—reaching across the aisle, sitting down over beers, and so on—may sound like a sensible approach (especially for social workers, whose training is built on developing listening and communication skills), but it is often a waste of time and energy. This is not to say that no one's mind can *ever* be changed. Sustained, nonjudgmental dialogue, even about complicated and contentious issues, can alter opinions under the right circumstances (Kalla and Broockman 2020), and one recent study suggests that op-eds might have significant and relatively long-lasting effects (Coppock, Ekins, and Kirby 2018).

You can see the troubling implications for political debate and dialogue and for informed voting and political decision making. It's tough to admit this, especially since there is an entire industry of politicians and political commentators who have built their careers on this cooperation/moderation/comity model (not to mention insidiously naïve cultural artifacts like *The West Wing*). Older readers might think of former columnist and commentator David Broder as an exemplar of this studied centrism, willingly blind to differences between the parties. David Brooks, among others, plays this game today in the pages of the *New York Times* (D. Roberts 2018). Some people feared that this is how President Biden would govern—offering paeans to bipartisanship that ignore the reality of how power is wielded and how change happens (or is thwarted) today. I understand why people might wish to live in such a world, but they do damage to their clients and to those they would advocate for if they do not disabuse themselves of this pernicious self-deceit. Effective national politics today is not about cooperation, it is about conflict, and change comes not from acts of persuasion but from successful exertions of strategic power (see chapter 23 and conclusion).

LESSONS FOR PRACTICE

This chapter has shared some key findings from behavioral economics and political psychology. There are other insights with even deeper relevance to those of us working with poor and otherwise vulnerable and insecure populations. Poverty creates stress, and long-term stress, we know, can have a negative impact on people's mental health (causing or exacerbating depression and anxiety) as well as their physical health (including high blood pressure and heart disease). But sustained stress like that associated with poverty and economic insecurity can also lead to cognitive overload, in which the brain's capacity to engage in rational decision making is altered. Thus, people under grave financial duress—who arguably may most need to be making sound decisions—may be least able to do so, potentially making bad circumstances even worse (Mullainathan and Shafir 2013). This dynamic can lead us as practitioners to fall into the trap of fundamental attribution error, in which we mistake behavior caused by systemic conditions or external forces beyond an individual's immediate control for behavior that reflects individual irresponsibility or immorality. There will be more to say in this vein in the next chapter. We might also, in this context, keep in mind the research discussed in chapter 11, in which we saw how the very operations of social welfare programs can teach people lessons about their worth and about the usefulness of political engagement. As you know, individual behavior can be a reflection of unseen forces or buried trauma, and our political systems can be among those sources of trauma, especially for populations who have been historically erased, exploited, or terrorized by them.

Chapter Twenty-Two

SOCIAL WORK IS CONSERVATIVE

OUR CONSTITUTIONAL system has failed us, and while we will continue here to explore the incremental interventions you can make within existing systems to achieve change at the local, state, or national level for your clients and your communities, we must, as a profession, also think bigger and embrace more disruptive and radical interventions to alter the increasingly corrupt, unjust, and undemocratic institutions under which we are governed. This will be a challenge, because social work has historically shied away from radical perspectives and solutions; it has in this way been generally conservative, a claim that may surprise you.

For some who seek to offer help to people in need, there's a blind spot that impedes their ability to intervene usefully. Bruce Jansson has described it as the "mythology of autonomous practice," which deludes social workers into thinking that "they and their clients are relatively insulated from external policies" and therefore don't need to attend to them (Popple and Leighninger 2001, 6). As he argues, this is wrong. You can't understand clients' problems without understanding the world in which they live, the actual constraints upon their actions, and their real range of choices. You are less likely to be able to help the person in front of you if you don't know something about both local and national politics, regulations and policy, community effects and neighborhood organization, intergovernmental relations, and more. Sociology, economics, and political science matter for good social service delivery just as much as psychology does— maybe even more.

Holding onto this mythology of autonomous practice can harm clients. If you reflexively think that solutions are rooted in altering the individual's behavior or attitudes, or in psychotherapy, you are likely to unthinkingly assume that the *causes* reside there too. The result can be that you look for individual-level explanations for problems instead of social or structural ones (Krumer-Nevo 2020). And, intentionally or not, you wind up blaming people for their state of need. This can persist even as person-in-environment and systems theories abound in social work education and practice.

Thinking of poverty as pathology is a long-standing problem. We see it in the age-old division between the *worthy* and *unworthy* poor, or the *deserving* and the *undeserving*. This is at the heart of the ideological debate about whether poverty is principally a problem of *culture* or *structure*. Is it the result of individual moral failings or the result of social and environmental forces? This debate was present at the birth of the social work profession in the late 1800s; it marks the divide between liberals like Mary Richmond or Homer Folks, conservatives such as Josephine Shaw Lowell and Stephen Humphreys Gurteen, and the genuine radicals like Florence Kelley, Lillian Wald, and Jane Addams. It's the liberals and the conservatives who gave birth to the profession and founded its first schools, while the radicals, including Addams, were Red-baited into penury and marginalized (Reisch and Andrews 2002; Pimpare 2004). Yet, ironically, it's the radicals that the profession is now inclined to name as its founders. To wit: In the lobby of a relatively new building at an East Coast school of social work, there is a mural-sized image of Addams and a quote from her about our obligations to each other: "The good we secure for ourselves is precarious and uncertain until it is secured for all of us and incorporated into our common life." But it's not the labor activism or municipal reform efforts of the Settlement Houses that sit at the heart of the curriculum there (or most anywhere, in my experience); rather, it is the nineteenth century's "Friendly Visitor" methods of casework, investigation, and social diagnosis, manifested today in efforts to treat systemic immiseration with cognitive behavioral therapy (Dalal 2018; Kim and Cardemil 2012).

The rhetorical heroes of the profession were policy practitioners, who blended original research into the conditions in the poorest neighborhoods with critical analysis, fierce advocacy, and committed, stubborn activism, all of which was inseparable from their service delivery (Schram 2002). They were not concerned with changing poor people so that they were better suited to thrive in the world but determined instead to change the world so that it better met the needs of the people who lived in it. But too many in the discipline today, with the *Diagnostic and Statistical Manual of Mental Disorders* (American Psychiatric Association 2013) in hand, treat human need as if it were, quite literally, a disease, a pathology, an inner sickness in need of a diagnosis followed by treatment, which is today governed by standards of "evidence-based practice" (Krumer-Nevo 2020).

This too is an old lament. Since the rise of Freud early in the twentieth century, there has been a contentious debate over whether there is too much psychology and not enough sociology in social work, whether the clinician and the counselor have supplanted the engaged activist, the researcher, and the reformer (Specht and Courtney 1995). There are many likely causes for this shift away from being out and engaged in the world toward more insular, individual treatment—the shift from trying to repair the world to fixing people. Some of this preoccupation with diagnosis and casework is to ensure that hours are billable to insurance companies; some is perhaps to avoid Addams's fate and not be tarred as a troublemaker (Addams became *persona non grata* and, with few exceptions, Settlement Houses exist today in name only); and some is likely in order to make the discipline more reputable and to overcome a long-standing inferiority complex (in the 1920s social work emulated medical schools—this is why there are internships—in order to legitimize it in the eyes of men) (Wenocur and Reisch 1989).

But genuine reformers are rarely reputable, because they almost inevitably are fighting against the status quo and entrenched power, and professionalization can be another word for co-optation. As with Martin Luther King, Jr., we may celebrate radicals, but we do it in a form that strips them of the very thoughts and deeds that made them dangerous and vilified in their time. We make them safe and nonthreatening. So, most of the MLK we get on his annual holiday is the "I Have a Dream" speech, not the King of "Letter from a Birmingham Jail" or the King who was organizing janitors and planning a national anti-poverty campaign when he was gunned down. We get twen-ty-foot-high celebrations of Jane Addams ministering to poor people, but not so much as a framed 8 x 10 of the labor agitator, the instigator, the vocal opponent of World War I, much less the socialist. We celebrate the accomplishments of the radical but erase from the record the means by which such achieve-ments came to be, giving students (and all of us) a distorted sense of how improvements to well-being came to pass.

Casework and clinical work, ministering one-on-one to people in need, is safer, but it is insufficient. Helping parents find food for their hungry children is vital work, literally, but if that's all you do, you're not furthering social justice and fulfilling your obligations under the NASW code. That requires you to act on a broader stage to effect systemic change so that instead of ameliorating the suffering before you, you're preventing it from happening in the first place. Wendy Jacobson, in an article called "Beyond Therapy" published in the flagship journal of the discipline, put it this way:

> Social workers make excellent clinical practitioners, and the profession should continue to train people for this work. However, therapy is not a particularly useful intervention for alleviating poverty, building sustainable communities, or generally improving outcomes for disadvantaged people. (Jacobson 2001)

This is a tension that goes back at least to the first professor of social policy, Richard Titmuss of the London School of Economics, who distinguished between residual and institutional programs, or the ameliorative versus the preventive. The residualist runs a canned-food drive to feed people. The institutionalist fights to eradicate the soup kitchen with broad, universal programs that distribute their benefits based not on categorical need but on one's status as a citizen or even as a human. This is not without risks, as Addams learned. Dom Hélder Camara, the so-called Bishop of the Slums, famously complained that "when I feed the poor they call me a saint, but when I ask why the poor have no food, they call me a communist." If you are fighting for more food for emergency feeding programs or offering counseling to those who show up there seeking help, and that's all that you are doing, the grim hunger statistics we face in the United States are unlikely to change. The reason is simple: The principal causes of need are not rooted in individual failure and are therefore not amenable to therapeutic intervention. Only political intervention will do.

The NASW Code of Ethics asserts:

> Social workers should engage in social and political action that seeks to ensure that all people have equal access to the resources, employment, services, and opportunities they require to meet their basic human needs and to develop fully. Social workers should be aware of the impact of the political arena on practice and should advocate for changes in policy and legislation to improve social conditions in order to meet basic human needs and promote social justice. (National Association of Social Workers 2017)

Despite this mandate and rhetorical support for activism and sometimes even radicalism, the evidence shows that social workers are often absent from the spaces where change happens. While social workers may vote at higher rates and be more likely to talk about politics and policy with their family and friends (which is all to the good, of course), most do not engage in community organizing, policy advocacy that extends beyond advocating for individual clients or narrowly for the profession, or electoral campaign activities—although such engagement is typically higher for Black social workers (Domanski 1998; Ezell 1993; Figueira-McDonough 1993; Mattocks 2018; Pritzker and Lane 2017; Rothman and Mizrahi 2014). As Margaret Dietz Domanski put it, "For social workers as a group to represent a potential participation threat to legislators, members of the profession must participate in numbers that are noticed" (Domanski 1998, 166), even if they may have concerns about their own qualifications or ability to effect change (Ostrander, Bryan, and Lane 2019).

It is perhaps not surprising that some people have increasingly called for social workers to replace some of the work currently done by police officers. But we should be wary of this precisely because we cannot count on social workers to be aligned with the weak over the strong (Leotti 2020). Police officers and social workers occupy similar bureaucratic spaces: they have enormous discretion in how they apply the rules in any individual case, creating opportunities for conscious and unconscious biases to play out in how they mete out benefits and punishment (Lipsky 2010). Cameron Rasmussen and Kirk James put it this way:

Social work's reckoning must include confronting our complicity in colonization, in racial capitalism and the logics of neoliberalism, and in our relationship to the carceral state, all of which have become core to social work practice . . . social workers have a long and troubled history as partners to the state, more often serving as carceral enforcers than as collaborators toward liberation. (Rasmussen and James 2020)

As Paolo Freire said, "It is impossible for a social worker to continue being progressive when she or he only talks progressive but acts conservative or reactionary" (Moch 2009, 95).

Social workers may idealize Addams, but they have not studied her carefully or taken her seriously, much less others like Mary Van Kleek, who opposed the New Deal from the Left (Ehrenreich 2014). Some have adopted a naive and idealized version of the Progressive Era's emphasis on the value of technocratic expertise, believing that educating policy makers and the public to sound and just policies would result in genuine forward-thinking change. In this view, injustice is a problem of education, communication, or public relations. There is little in our history to suggest that this is the case. This belief in the transformative power of the rational argument or the moral appeal is especially pernicious in social work education. This is another, equally dangerous kind of American Exceptionalism and one that would seem to be especially futile in an era that gave new life to "fake news," white supremacists in the White House, ignorant and inexperienced officials scattered throughout all levels of the federal government, and a broad-based disdain for education, expertise, and reason.

LESSONS FOR PRACTICE

Recognize the power and the ongoing resistance of marginalized peoples. Don't try to fix them—they are not broken. Instead, seek ways to help them to activate their power and to alter the systems and structures that harm, constrain, and kill them. As Michal Krumer-Nevo (2020) puts it, "develop an ethic of solidarity." You must recognize that people are in a state of constant resistance even if that resistance takes forms that are hard for you to see (Scott 2000). Abandon the notion that poor people are passive and abandon the idea that it is their attitude or behavior that causes their poverty; simultaneously, cast aside any notion that you are necessarily morally or intellectually superior. Instead of "empathy," says Krumer-Nevo, speak of "solidarity," and instead of "strengths," speak of "agency." It is also worth contemplating why recent research finds new evidence of the "thick skin bias," which leads people to think that poor people are more resilient to adverse life circumstances and emotional pain and therefore less affected by them—and the fact that this phenomenon is no less present in social workers than it is in others (Cheek and Shafir 2020).

Given all this, you might look for ways to engage in "therapeutic advocacy" or "active right exercising." For example, "accompanying clients to encounters with various bureaucratic agents not only fulfills real social needs . . . but also serves to create a space for the unique voice of the clients, which is frequently silenced by destructive social power structures" (Krumer-Nevo 2020, 159). That is, use your position and power strategically. Accompany your client to important meetings with other agents of the state, but not so that you can speak for them; rather, join them so that you can use your power to insist that they be able to speak for themselves. And take their pain seriously; do not conclude that their hardships are not so bad because they are used to them.

You can also think more critically about the systems you are complicit in. Do you trust the processes that will take over once you pass along a report after a home visit? If you do not know those systems well and cannot answer with a clear and certain "yes," then perhaps you need to think twice. I realize that this goes against your training, and in many cases against the law. I make no recommendation here other than that you think carefully about the nature of the problem—or the perceived problem—you are confronting and that you think carefully about your response, recognizing the reality that you could make things worse rather than better by being an active participant in unjust, racist, dysfunctional systems of control masquerading as systems of assistance (Stevenson, Bottoms, and Burke 2020). This is why there is growing recognition that there is almost no problem in the United States today that cannot be made worse by involving the police, especially in communities of color; think about this maxim as you think about what happens when you call in Child Protective Services. On whose behalf are you using your power? How do you wield your discretion? How can you alter those systems for the betterment of your clients, their families, and their neighborhoods?

Chapter Twenty-Three

THROW SAND IN THE GEARS
OF EVERYTHING

POLICY KNOWLEDGE matters for effective practice. Simplistic views of the political process can foster unrealistic expectations among on-the-ground workers about the possibility for social progress. Too many enter the profession hopeful and idealistic and determined to make change but are then confronted with a daunting array of formidable obstacles, including entrenched bureaucracies peopled with petty functionaries and a Byzantine political system. They then become discouraged and overwhelmed and suffer cynicism, depression, and burnout.

To help avoid this, you need to form a three-dimensional portrait of how change has happened in the past and, just as important, how and why it hasn't happened; you then need to identify your own goals and sketch out a practicable path for achieving them while tracking your progress toward those goals and measuring your direct and indirect successes and setbacks.

Some talk about this as having a theory of change (Coryn et al. 2011; Organizational Research Services 2004; Farmelo 2015).

Political and policy changes do not happen easily, and they do not generally happen because ideas change but because power relations change. The history of U.S. social-welfare policy suggests that only when large groups of previously marginalized people press against the system, threatening physical disruption or electoral disorder, can our institutions which were designed to resist innovation, be forced to act, to move, and to respond (Piven 2006). No significant political progress has occurred over the course of U.S. history that did not have at its heart disruptive protest that pushed from outside the system—often rudely, outrageously, and angrily.

As Reverend King put it in his "Letter from a Birmingham Jail," "we know through painful experience that power is never given voluntarily by the oppressor, it must be demanded by the oppressed" (King 1963). Those aligned with Occupy Wall Street knew this. So do those working under the Black Lives Matter banner. This is just as it was in the 1930s and the 1960s. There is no satisfying explanation of the New Deal or Great Society "big bangs" of policy advancement without an account of the role played by mass mobilizations—protests, strikes, marches, and the like (Piven and Cloward 1979).

While the disruptive elements of protest may be necessary for it to achieve change, the disruption is not the point; it is merely the means to an end, often the only form of leverage available to people being ignored by or excluded from the "normal" configurations of electoral politics, lobbying, and interest-group pressure. That was King's point: He and his compatriots couldn't get a seat at the table, so they had to create a crisis to get those in power to even consider their demands—demands that were, as with most movement demands, not especially radical in retrospect. They wanted the nation to abide by the Constitution (as amended) and the law and to treat Black Americans as full citizens and as people worthy of dignity and respect. In this way, we depend upon the radicals to open up spaces for moderate change.

To be effective, those disruptions must be strategic. One useful way to think about this is through Frances Fox Piven's notion of interdependence. We all exist within complex webs of mutual dependence, she observes: We depend on our employers for wages, but our employers also depend on us for our labor. We depend on our local grocery store for food and supplies for our family, and the store depends on our business to keep its doors open. We depend on our mayors to ensure that the roads are plowed and that the water is clean, and they depend on us for votes. Each party to each of those relationships is necessary, and in each instance, the power we have is the threat to withdraw our contribution: to stop going to work or to go on strike; to boycott the local store; to vote for the challenger. For people without other sources of power and influence, their power lies in their ability to withdraw their passive acceptance of injustice—that is, to go from being quiet and obedient to being loud and disruptive (Piven 2006; Piven and Cloward 1966).

This kind of analysis is an important part of developing your own theory of change. What is the source of *your* leverage? What contribution are you making to an oppressive system, and can you withdraw it in order to reveal and activate your power? What are the forces that will cause your targets to comply or resist?

One study of the civil rights movement shows that many Southern businesses only complied with the Civil Rights Act of 1964—which prohibited race-based discrimination in employment, voter registration, and public accommodations—because their livelihoods (unlike schools or election administration) were directly affected by targeted protest; in fact, in order to minimize the impact of protest, some segregated businesses even worked to encourage their cities to desegregate—not because they cared about racial justice or equality but because they wanted the controversy to go away and to escape responsibility for complying or not complying (Luders 2010).

Disruptions need to be targeted, but they also need to be . . . well . . . disruptive. Shutting down a highway, occupying a lunch counter, boycotting a store or bus line, refusing en masse to show up for work, or picketing the entrance to a business—each of these tactics has potential for effectiveness only because the party withdrawing its participation in the relationship upends the normal order (Piven 2006). If you hear people complaining about protesters' tactics and how they are inconvenienced by them, that may be a sign that the insurgents are doing something right. Look for spaces where you might have disruptive leverage and then, as Piven put it when thinking through how to resist the Trump administration, "throw sand in the gears of everything" (Piven 2017).

But remember that there is no guarantee that disruptive protest will succeed. The target may offer concessions, as you would hope, but they may ignore the movement activity (if they can, they will), or they may meet the movement with violence and repression, as we discussed briefly in chapter 4 (Piven and Cloward 1979).

A movement can serve as an essential impetus for policy change, but it can also change attitudes or emerge from changing attitude and ideas. As activist and scholar Angela Davis noted:

> Regimes of racial segregation were not disestablished because of the work of leaders and presidents and legislators but rather because of the fact that ordinary people adopted a critical stance in the way in which they perceived their relationship to reality. Social realities that may have appeared inalterable, impenetrable, came to be viewed as malleable and transformable; and people learned how to imagine what it might mean to live in a world that was not so exclusively governed by the principle of white supremacy. This collective consciousness emerged within the context of social struggles. (Davis 2013)

Those effects can be long-lasting. One study found that "whites from counties that experienced civil rights protests over 50 years ago are less likely to harbor racial resentment against African Americans, more likely to support affirmative action, and more likely to identify as Democrats today" (Mazumder 2018).

There is a second way that change happens, and that is through a kind of incrementalism. The original old-age insurance benefit created in the Social Security Act of 1935 was a modest program that excluded broad swaths of the population and paid paltry benefits. Only after a series of hard-fought amendments, including those in 1939 (adding dependent and survivors' benefits), 1950 (expanding coverage to previously excluded categories of workers and increasing benefit levels), 1954 (adding coverage for self-employed workers), 1956 (creating its disability program), 1961 and 1962 (expanding access to AFDC), and 1973 (creating SSI) did it become the nearly universal pension scheme we know it as today. Knowledge of how such incremental—but ultimately profound—changes came about can help plot effective strategies for policy change today (Béland 2007; Social Security Administration n.d.).

Another, perhaps more practical, reason for this knowledge is to attain a sophisticated understanding of the panoply of forces—social, cultural, political, and economic—that combine to pinion poor and otherwise marginalized people, constraining their options. The more you come to understand how change has happened in the past, and why it's so rare, the more you can come to accept the difficulty of effecting positive social change today. MLK famously said that the arc of history is long but that it bends toward justice. I agree, at least on my optimistic days, but the arc is *very* long, and it can sometimes seem to be getting longer rather than shorter. Progress is possible—but so is regress.

Change is difficult, and it typically requires regular, sustained effort over extended periods of time. Consider that most Democratic presidents since FDR tried to enact a program of universal health care, but only in 2010, with the passage of the Affordable Care Act (ACA), do we see something we might call success. And what the ACA created is at best (as Social Security was) a foundation—the beginning of a process of extending access to health care for all of us, not its culmination—especially as governors and state legislatures resist, as Congress and the Trump administration tried to pull it apart and defund it, and as courts continue to rule on its constitutionality. There is and will continue to be much hard work to come, which can be frustrating and dispiriting, given how exhausting the original battles were. But anyone interesting in effecting change on behalf of marginalized populations has got to make their peace with that.

Max Weber wrote in 1919:

> Politics is a strong and slow boring of hard boards. It takes both passion and perspective. Certainly all historical experience confirms the truth—that Man would not have attained the possible unless time and again he had reached out for the impossible. (Weber [1919] 1965)

It's good advice, even a century later. Action, not ideas, is what matters, but you must persist. Social change is a life's work, and it will come slowly. But it will come, if you persist and persist strategically. That means knowing where to exert pressure on the system, and when, and how to sustain it. As Rev. William J. Barber II, leader of the modern Poor People's Campaign, put it:

> Down through history, we've never won anything with one march, one tweet, one speech—that is a misreading of history. We've always won progressive and revolutionary growth in this country through campaigns. Through 381 days of having a Montgomery bus boycott, for example, or through

years of the abolition movement. Persistence in a movement is a ritual you must have. You must have a deep commitment to civil disobedience and be willing to put your bodies on the line in a nonviolent way, rooted in love and justice, to dramatize the ugliness of what's going on. (Losier and Barber 2019)

LESSONS FOR PRACTICE

Remember, no one is coming to save you. Don't get trapped by the collective action problem (Olson 2003): believing that you don't need to act because someone else will or that your participation won't make much difference, or any difference at all. That may be true, but if everyone thinks that, then no one acts, nothing gets done, and nothing changes. It's not enough to find ways to express solidarity with clients (Krumer-Nevo 2020); you must also think about how you can help them mobilize—how to identify the sources of their own power and then to express it and activate it. Can you identify the places in which you have power, in which you have leverage? Can you name the contribution you are making to the interdependent relationship at issue and identify how to disrupt it? What is the plan for that disruption? How will you activate your power?

CONCLUSION

WE CAN DO BETTER. THERE ARE SOLUTIONS.

LIFE IS hard. Family is hard. Work is hard, and you have already joined a profession that may pay you less and stress you more than if you had made other choices. Isn't just being a social worker enough? No, it is not, I'm afraid. As you know, the NASW Code of Ethics imposes obligations upon you. More than that, because of the specialized insight you likely possess about vulnerable populations, what causes them harm, and what could most readily improve their well-being, you have a particular obligation to share that knowledge and to press the political system to do something about it. You could do this for selfish reasons, too: How much easier would your job be if your clients' lives weren't quite so difficult? If they were not quite so vulnerable? If they had a bit more safety and security? Finally, and perhaps more to the point: If not you, then who?

In the preface to this book, I asked if there were lessons to be learned from the events of 2020 that could help us design and execute effective strategies for social action and policy change. The novel coronavirus pandemic revealed the fractures in and failures of the U.S. political system and its programs of social support, laying bare the effects of decades of systematic antigovernment rhetoric and disinvestment in public institutions, rampant and rising inequality, and accumulated disadvantage heaped especially on Black, brown, and Native peoples and their communities. For our purposes, the question becomes how we can increase the power and the resilience of more people so that when the next crisis hits—and there is always a next crisis—they are less vulnerable to it. Recent events have shown that the things people have been telling us are impossible or unsolvable are neither. That should be a source of hope. The U.S. political system can, in fact, do big things quickly when it wants to. Part of the challenge we face is how to make it want to.

With the electoral defeat of Donald Trump, you may be tempted to breathe a sigh of relief and go back to ignoring politics until the next election. But as I have noted throughout these pages, the problem with U.S. political and policy-making systems predated Trump and runs deeper than any one individual or regime.

What can you do? Beyond what you can find in the Lessons for Practice sections in the previous chapters, here are some additional thoughts on how you might begin to organize your thinking and your planning for sustained action and civic engagement.

BUILD KNOWLEDGE

Many of you are reading this book because you are enrolled in an undergraduate or graduate program in social work. That means that you are already working to acquire the knowledge and skills to help improve the well-being of the populations you care most about. But remember that your formal education is the start of a process, not its end. It is my hope that this book has made you a more critical thinker about matters of politics and policy and that you will build upon that foundation moving forward. Now, however, that general knowledge needs to be supplemented by more specialized mastery of your own areas of concern and interest. What can you do to continue to acquire and maintain useful knowledge?

- For general information about political issues of the day, read broadly across multiple sources. The more regularly you do this, the better you will be at identifying those outlets that are making an effort to give you useful information and the context to help you make sense of it. Do not use your television for political news—broadcasters are interested in creating drama so that you stay tuned and see their advertising, not in helping you become a better or smarter citizen.
- Find informed, reliable sources that regularly report on the particular issues or populations you care about. Look at the websites of organizations doing work in your areas and see if they have a "research" or "policy reports" section. If they have a regular newsletter or podcast, sign up or subscribe to it; an easy way to keep up to date is to have

groups that you know and trust "push" information to you. If you carefully curate your feed, you can get Twitter to function this way for you too.

• Identify dependable web sources and create a folder in your browser so that they are all in one place; make multiple folders if there are more issues or populations on which you want to keep current. If you care about health policy, for example, you might start with regular visits to Kaiser Family Foundation State Health Facts (kff.org/statedata) to learn about what's going on near you, or evaluate your state Medicaid program to help identify local needs and shape your advocacy (www.cbpp.org/evaluating-your-state-medicaid -program#restrictions). Set aside a little time every week to check these sites for new information.

• Make sure you know who all of your elected representatives are at the national, state, and local level. You can easily find out who most of them are here: ballotpedia. org/Who_represents_me.

• Find the bills moving through Congress and set up alerts for those you want to keep track of here: govtrack.us /congress/bills/.

• Go to your state legislature to search for bills there; here's the excellent site for the state where I live: gencourt.state. nh.us/bill_Status/. Find your own state legislature here: www.congress.gov/state-legislature-websites.

• Know how the policy-making process works in your city and state. Again, here's what's readily available about mine: www.manchesternh.gov/Government, www .nh.gov/almanac/bills.htm.

- Look up the voting record of your representatives: ballot-pedia.org/Lifetime_voting_records_of_United_States_Senators_and_Representatives.
- Discover which people and interests have funded their election campaigns: opensecrets.org/influence/.
- Understand the demographic makeup of your area. What can you learn about the education, income, and racial background of people who live there? census.gov/data.html.
- Compare what you learn about people's income in your area with what it costs to meet a family's basic needs: livingwage.mit.edu/.
- Consider how likely it is that you (or someone you know) will be poor: confrontingpoverty.org/poverty-risk-calculator/.
- See where your own politics lie or with whom your policy priorities align. Go to I Side With . . . (www.isidewith.com/), the Political Compass (politicalcompass.org), or the Pew Research Center's Political Typology Quiz (pewresearch.org/politics/quiz/political-typology/).
- Review the bibliography of this book for further reading in areas of your particular interest.

BUILD STRATEGY

Knowledge without action is of limited use or impact.

- What will you do with your knowledge? What is the issue that most concerns you? What are the biggest obstacles in the way of better outcomes? Where are the decisions made? In the mayor's office? A city or state agency? The state legislature? Where, specifically, within those institutions? Which subcommittee? Which bureaucrat? You can't make change if you don't know where to direct your efforts.

- Like good therapeutic interventions, good advocacy will follow basic principles and practices but is always unique to the circumstances; it differs from issue to issue, place to place, and time to time. Advocacy must always be context specific.

- Change does not typically come from "one-off" efforts but is more typically the culmination of many years, or even decades, of consistent work. Think about how you want to incorporate your advocacy or activism into your daily or weekly routine. As you build networks of solidarity, develop a reputation as someone who is informed (and listens and learns when you are not), reliable (you do what you say you will do and show up when you are expected to), and working for the betterment of the group or the community.

- Focus less on national politics—where you are likely to have less influence—and more on state and local politics, where you can have a real impact. That doesn't mean that you should ignore national politics, but recognize that you have limited time and energy. Spend them where they have the greatest chance of mattering.

- Be ready to seize the opening of a policy window—that moment when, for one reason or another, large portions of the policy-making apparatus are focused on the same issue and feel compelled to act. The attacks of September 11, 2001, the financial crisis that started in 2008, and the coronavirus pandemic fall into this category. On the local level, when a child who is in foster care or in the child protective services system dies, a policy window often opens as attention is drawn to the issue and many different actors press for change. It may seem cynical or morbid to take advantage of those awful circumstances to advance your preferred policy reform, but that moment is precisely the time to press your advantage; it's when you probably have the best chance of preventing the next tragedy. Shrewd advocates are always ready for a policy window to open unexpectedly so that they can attach their preferred solution to the current problem; these spaces of "organized anarchy" can open up surprising opportunities for change for the clever policy entrepreneur (Kingdon 2011; Cohen, March, and Olsen 1972).

- As you think about timing and strategy, think also about budgets and budget cycles. These are regular and predicable policy windows when you know that much of the system will be engaged in considering how to allocate resources among a wide range of competing demands and interests. Especially if your needs are financially modest, this may be a good opportunity to slip funding into a larger bill where the big fights are over other, more expensive budget lines. The National League of Cities (www .nlc.org/resources/type/fact-sheet/) and the National Conference of State Legislatures (www.ncsl.org/research

/fiscal-policy/budget-cycle.aspx) have good resources available. Do you know what your agency's annual budget is and where to find it? What about your city or town's budget? The way to really understand an organization's values is not through the rhetoric its leaders use but in how it allocates its resources: The budget shows you what really matters.

- While you are thinking about local budgets, think about ways to implement participatory budgeting. This looks different in different places, but this now decades-old practice turns over all or some of the budgeting decisions to community groups (Lerner 2014). In New York City, for example, where each member of the city council has a pot of discretionary funds that they are allowed to spend in their districts, many members have given those decisions to residents. For more information on such projects, see participatorybudgeting.org and council.nyc.gov/pb/.

- One of the lessons that the coronavirus pandemic taught us is that crisis creates unexpected spaces for policy change (see the preface to this book). This is a lesson for the local and agency level too. Look around at the institutional spaces you inhabit and see if you can get permanent policy changes enacted along with any pandemic emergency measures that were put in place (or actions that are taken in response to any new emergency). If your organization relaxed its rules around sick days, for example, or offered paid leave for the first time, that would have been a great time to ask why such things should be available only in time of widespread crisis when individual people

CONCLUSION

and families have crises all the time. If someone tells you
that "now is not the time," this often indicates that it is
precisely the time. Keep in mind that once the pandemic
subsides (if it hasn't already by the time you are reading
this), there will be efforts to roll back those emergency
policies. Take a look now at the ones you would like to
remain permanent, and start building a plan for waging
and winning that fight or for reinstating the best of the
emergency programs that were allowed to expire.

- As you think about changes to policies you believe to be
  badly designed, harmful, or irrational, remember the lessons
  of chapter 8: consider the possibility that those policies
  exist because someone benefits from them. Always strive to
  uncover the possible deeper logic of the policy at hand and
  build your own plan with these dynamics in mind.

- Similarly, construct your proposed new policies or alterations to existing ones with feedback effects in mind (see
  chapter 9). What new spaces does your policy change
  create for future contests over the policy? Whom does
  it advantage? If what you can achieve now is insufficient
  to the problem, how can you structure this more limited
  alteration so that it will serve as a solid foundation for
  future improvements?

- Remember that most change results from a combination
  of insider and outsider power. In many instances, there
  need to be people pressing from outside the formal
  policy-making arena to insist upon action, force policy
  makers to act, and then hold them accountable. In the
  recent words of two organizers, "We can't just elect our

way to a better world. We have to build a bottom-up movement that can change the conditions in which elected officials make decisions, and force policies that benefit the vast majority of people and the planet" (Day and Uetricht 2020, 109). But there also need to be people within the system who are open to that kind of pressure and persuasion and who will ultimately respond to it. We cannot focus solely on social movement activity or on electoral and legislative politics—we must do both (although each of us individually may choose to do our work on only one side of this equation).

- If you are working from outside the system to create pressure on it, there are lots of ways to go about that work. One place to jump-start your thinking is with the Albert Einstein Institution's 198 Methods of Nonviolent Action: aeinstein.org/nonviolentaction/198-methods-of -nonviolent-action/.

- If the work you are doing is better located within the "normal" policy-making system, there are lots of good area-specific guides and more general books for legislative advocacy (Hoefer 2019; Richan 2006; Rocha 2007; Cummins, Byers, and Pedrick 2011; Carroll 2011).

- In either instance, you will likely want to build a media strategy too. The "Media Advocacy" chapter of the Community Toolbox (ctb.ku.edu/en/table-of-contents) is an excellent place to begin. But don't just try to reach people during a crucial moment of protest or stage of policy making; work to build an audience over time, which increases the chances that when you do have a message that you want to circulate further, that you might be able to do it. Remember: it's a slow and steady boring of hard boards.

- Look for opportunities to elevate the voices of others who have insight, experience, or knowledge that you do not. This is another way to build trust, build your network, and build your own knowledge at the same time.

- Do not settle on a policy agenda or develop strategies to enact it in a vacuum. The model of participatory action research encourages scholars and others interested in producing policy research to start by having conversations with local organizations and residents and allowing them to define what their own needs are (Adams 2019; Schram 2002; Shdaimah, Stahl, and Schram 2011).

- As you do that work, remember a basic principle of asset-based community development: identify plans for your communities by mapping assets, not needs (M. Green et al. 2006). That is, apply the principles you know as strengths-based approaches in your clinical work to your community and advocacy work too. You will find that there are enormous resources already available within any group undertaking advocacy work; if you can effectively identify them and then help marshal them to action, you will have much better chances of success.

BUILD COMMUNITY

No matter how deep your knowledge or how sound your plans, it is unlikely that you will be able to effect even modest change alone. Enduring change is made by groups of people working toward common purpose.

- Your starting place should be first to find people who are already doing the work on the issues you care about and to join them.
- If you find that there really are no groups already doing the things you want to do, it's still advisable to find ways to tap into existing networks. Who's doing work on similar issue areas or in the same geographical region? Reach out to them, tell them what you are interested in, and ask them to share their knowledge, experience, and advice with you. Try to do more listening than talking.
- If you are not sure whether networks of potential allies already exist, reach out to your state-level NASW chapter (https://www.socialworkers.org/About/Chapters/Find-a-Chapter). Also see if they have a Political Action for Candidate Election (PACE) arm.
- While you are reaching out, think about how you can be more involved with their work. What skills do you have that you can share? Do you have networks or connections that could help them? What work are you willing to do?
- Can you find a legislative committee that works on the policy areas or population groups that most concern you and listen in on their meetings? Just being more knowledgeable about and engaged in state and local issues helps you, your clients, and your communities.

- Similarly, find out about the local political party organizations in your city or state. They will likely have regular meetings where you can learn about upcoming local campaigns or pressing community needs. This is also a place where getting involved might be very easy, since local political parties are often desperate for people to step up and assume roles. This kind of work can be a gateway for becoming involved in campaigns or even deciding to run for a local office yourself.
- Don't neglect the work that is likely going on through local churches, synagogues, and mosques.
- A related way to build communities and to create networks is to find ways to be useful to people; creating relationships of mutual aid and interdependence fosters the kinds of solidarity and trust that can then be directed at institutions of power for the betterment of the community. In the words of Dean Spade, whose short book *Mutual Aid* is an indispensable, accessible primer on the subject, mutual aid is "survival work, when done in conjunction with social movements demanding transformative change" (Spade 2020, 1). What distinguishes mutual aid from mere charity is that broader focus: people come together to help each other, often in times of crisis; through that work, they build analyses of the systems that created the problems they face and then develop action to transform them. Unlike social service agencies that may appear at first glance to be doing similar work, mutual aid is typically antihierarchical

and "inherently anti-authoritarian, demonstrating how we can do things together in ways we were told not to imagine" (Spade 2020, 16). The Big Door Brigade (http://bigdoorbrigade.com/) is another source of information about mutual aid.

- Community organizing can also take the form of more traditional organization building and activism. Here, too, there are excellent resources and guides from people who have devoted years and decades to doing the work (Minieri and Getsos 2007; Bobo, Kendall, and Max 2010).

- An exceptional resource for thinking through the nuts and bolts and step-by-step work of building networks, organizations, and movements of allies and colleagues is the Community Toolbox, run by the University of Kansas Center for Community Health and Development (https://ctb.ku.edu/en). There you will find a free, comprehensive guide to undertaking community assessments, engaging in strategic planning, thinking through organizational and leadership management challenges, fundraising, marketing, and more.

- Remember that all of this is work. As one political scientist put it, "People are not born with the capacity they need to engage in public life; it must be cultivated" (H. Han 2020, 6). But you may have more time for this than you think. How much time each day do you spend consuming media and social media? How else might you use some of that time?

BUILD POWER

With knowledge, strategy, and networks of like-minded people, you can then take action. As I have said, it is useful and important to keep up to date on political news and on policy-specific news about issues and populations that you most care about; but do not mistake information gathering, petition signing, or making the occasional contribution—"hobbyism"—for activism. Political scientist Eitan Hersh cautions:

> Of Americans who consume news every day, most report belonging to zero organizations. 65 percent report that in the last year they have done no work with other people to solve a community problem. 68 percent say they have attended zero meetings in the last year about a community issue. The population that is informed enough and cares enough about politics to follow the daily news is mostly disengaged from participation in political and community endeavors. . . . The average college-educated respondent says that 41 percent of the time he or she spends on politics is news consumption, 26 percent is discussing with friends and family either on social media or off-line, 21 percent is spent thinking about politics by themselves, 10 percent is in some way unclassifiable, and under 2 percent is in volunteering. (Hersh 2020, 136, 143–44)

Organizing, mobilization, and mutual aid are where the work of transformative political change is taking place. It is the sustained mass mobilizations of Black Lives Matter that changed racial politics in 2020, not another *Atlantic* article or a clever meme on Facebook. In the words of radical educator Paolo Freire, "Society is transformed when we transform it, and we transform it when the organized and mobilized political forces of the popular classes and workers throw themselves into history to change the world, and not in someone's head" (Moch 2009, 96).

So, think about ways you and your networks can take action to help achieve your goals and the goals of your brothers and sisters.

- Vote—in each and every election where you live, after you have taken some time to learn about the candidates and issues on the ballot—and get others to do the same. This work begins long before any election. Find people who are not registered to vote, talk to them about how and why their participation matters, and foster their engagement in politics and policies that affect them, so that when the next election comes around, they will not only vote but join you in helping to get other people to the polls. The more that your community can be expected to show up at the polls, the more likely are the people who depend upon your votes to listen to your concerns and act on them.

- Contribute. Elected official needs two things: votes and money. Let candidates know that you and your neighbors can give them both of those things—or refuse to do so. Your contributions do not need to be large—any amount allows you to call yourself a donor. Becoming a contributor will get you on mailing lists and newsletters, which can be an easy way to keep up on the issues that those elected officials are paying attention to.

- Call your elected officials, and get their other constituents to do the same (other people's elected officials probably don't much care what you think). Let them know that you are a constituent (they may ask for your address); you may also want to let them know that you are a financial supporter. Call them when you want them to vote a particular way, to complain that they voted the wrong way, and to thank them for voting the right way. Is there an issue that you think should be on their radar but is not? Call them and let them know. Do you have a compelling story from your practice that highlights a local problem? Share it. In almost every elected official's office, there is a tally sheet of one kind or another that tracks how many calls are coming into the office and what those callers are concerned about. If enough people make themselves heard, it will absolutely draw more attention to the issue.

- Alternatively, you can send an email or even a traditional letter by mail. Avoid form letters, though; precisely because they require less effort and thought on your part, they carry less weight. As a shorthand, assume that the less effort it takes for you to do something, the less impact it is likely to have. Is there any harm in circulating or signing petitions? In most instances, no. Is that likely to have much of an effect? Also no.

- Lobby in person. If you are a constituent, call your representative's office and ask if you can schedule a meeting with the officeholder or a staff member to talk about your issue. Bring a friend or colleague for moral support and to help make sure you make your points. Prepare what you want to say, keeping in mind that if you do get a meeting it will likely not be for more than a few minutes, and it's always a good idea to have a one-page overview of your main points that you can leave behind. Do not feel as if you are intruding or wasting their time; remember that their job is, literally, to represent you and that you may possess knowledge or insight that will help them make better decisions for their constituents.

- Testify. In my own state legislature, anyone can show up to any public committee hearing on any bill and sign up to speak briefly for or against it; this may be true on your state or city as well. As with in-person lobbying, this is a good way to show that you and your group care so much about the issue that you are willing to take the time and effort to make your preferences heard. This can also be good way to meet more like-minded people, and you can often learn a lot by seeing who is speaking on the other side of your bill and hearing what they have to say.

- If there are local radio programs that create space for conversations about the issues you care about, call in and make your case; think about what you could ask listeners to do with the information you share.

- Similarly, you could write an op-ed—a short opinion piece for publication in a local newspaper or online forum. Keep it brief, use accessible language, make it compelling, and let readers know what they should do. There are many good guides online; you might start with this one from the Indivisible Project: www.indivisible.org /resource/writing-opeds-make-difference.

- Join. Are there local organizations doing work you care about? Start attending their meetings and see if there is a way you can help advance the cause.

- Protest. This can take many forms—picket lines, rallies, marches, building takeovers, teach-ins, packing a hearing, street theater, boycotts, and more (Minieri and Getsos 2007)—but as you think about what form your action should take, remember chapter 23 and Piven's framework: Where do you have interdependent power? How can you exert that leverage? Attention for attention's sake often gets you little. What's the strategic use of collective action in the particular instance at hand?

- Run for something. Consider whether there is a position in which you could even more directly influence policy making. Remember that the more local the office (school board, zoning committee, community board), the greater the opportunities for you to step into office. This is an excellent way to get a feel for what it's like to be inside the system and to build the skills and connections that might lead you to higher offices.

- In all instances, think more about exerting power or leverage than about persuasion.

- Continue to make sure that you are advocating *with* marginalized populations, not *for* them.

BUILD RESILIENCE

You likely know from your training and experience about the important of regimens of self-care. This is especially important for those of you who work with people who have suffered physical or sexual abuse and have been traumatized by those experience. Finding ways not to let yourself be immobilized by such emotionally difficult work and to remain actively engaged in the face of brutality, suffering, and horror is part of what makes social work training so important. Without it, who would be left to do this important service without burning out? Political and policy advocacy is no different. As I have been at pains to emphasize, making change in the United States is difficult under the best of circumstances, and it is never the best of circumstances. Thus, finding ways to protect ourselves and maintain our commitment to the struggle is essential. Here are a few things you might keep in mind.

- "Hope is a discipline," organizer and activist Miriame Kaba (2021, 26) tells us. If you are to be optimistic about the possibility of change, you must practice that optimism. Internalize the belief that what you do matters and that it can and will succeed. Do this because it does, and it will. How do I know? Because such efforts have not only succeeded in the past but have been at the heart of every significant reform in our history. Remember the words often attributed to anthropologist Margaret Meade: "Never doubt that a small group of thoughtful, committed citizens can change the world: Indeed, it's the only thing that ever has."

- Celebrate your successes, no matter how small they are or how slight they may seem. A victory is a victory; let each and every one of them feed you and fuel you and your colleagues, friends, and neighbors, and draw on that energy to plan and carry out your next battle.
- By the same token, you must take time to mourn your losses. A defeat, especially on an issue you have devoted lots of time and energy to, can be crushing. It's okay to feel sad, dispirited, angry, or frustrated. Sit in that feeling for a while, and give everyone permission to grieve. Then perform an autopsy. Figure out what went wrong and why. Is there anything you could have done differently? Anything your strategy didn't account for? Stakeholders whose power you underestimated? Strengths on your side that you overestimated? Learn from this, and start thinking about how it will make you better prepared for the next battle. Then move on.
- Be patient; remember that "politics is a strong and slow boring of hard boards" (Weber [1919] 1965). Political progress typically comes from applying intense pressure over long periods of time to systems that are resistant to change. The work of the Black civil rights movement that culminated in the Civil Rights Act of 1964 and the Voting Rights Act of 1965 had its roots in the organizing work of Black churches beginning in the 1920s (McAdam 1999). Strong and slow boring of hard boards.

- Moderate your expectations. Progress is difficult to achieve and slow in coming; you will likely suffer many defeats before your first victory, more setbacks than successes. Expect to lose more than you win, remembering that the U.S. political and policy-making systems are stubbornly resistance to change, especially change that would benefit groups without ingrained power and influence.

- Set modest, achievable goals to avoid setting yourself up for unnecessary disappointment and to maximize the chances that you will have things to celebrate. Your goal can be the elimination of homelessness, but let that be the lifelong mission. In the interim, set realistic, small-bore steps that keep you on a path toward the larger goal (e.g., expand the number of available emergency shelter beds by 20 percent this winter).

- Find sources of inspiration to keep you going. They might be people you admire (both those you know and whose work you see as a model and ancestors you appreciate and respect), movements that have made achievements you celebrate, organizations whose ethics and practice you want to emulate, or case studies of advocacy campaigns that help you think through your own efforts.

- Remember your clinical skills and apply them: Be patient, be empathetic, listen; look for evidence-based approaches. Practice care for communities as you would for individuals.

- Laugh. Have fun. There is much joy to be found in working in common cause with others, even (or especially?)

on very serious issues. As activist Emma Goldman (may have) said, "If I can't dance, I don't want to be in your revolution."

• Former U.S. House member and civil rights activist John Lewis had useful advice in this regard: "Do not get lost in a sea of despair. Be hopeful, be optimistic. Our struggle is not the struggle of a day, a week, a month, or a year, it is the struggle of a lifetime. Never, ever be afraid to make some noise and get in good trouble, necessary trouble" (Lewis 2018).

Now, put down this book and go figure out what kind of trouble you want to get into.

REFERENCES

Abramovitz, Mimi. 2001. "Everyone Is Still on Welfare: The Role of Redistribution in Social Policy." *Social Work* 46 (4): 297–308. https://doi.org/10.1093/sw/46.4.297.

Achen, Christopher H., and Larry M. Bartels. 2017. *Democracy for Realists: Why Elections Do Not Produce Responsive Government: With a New Afterword by the Authors.* Princeton, NJ: Princeton University Press.

ACLU. 2020. "Block the Vote: Voter Suppression in 2020." American Civil Liberties Union. https://www.aclu.org/news/civil-liberties/block-the-vote-voter-suppression-in-2020/.

Adams, Danielle R. 2019. "Social Work's Role in Collaborative Community–Academic Partnerships: How Our Past Informs Our Future." *Social Work* 64 (1): 19–28. https://doi.org/10.1093/sw/swy046.

Aldrich, John Herbert. 1995. *Why Parties? The Origin and Transformation of Political Parties in America.* Chicago: University of Chicago Press.

Alinsky, Saul David. 1971. *Rules for Radicals: A Practical Primer for Realistic Radicals.* New York: Random House.

Alston, Philip. 2017. "Statement on Visit to the USA, by Professor Philip Alston, United Nations Special Rapporteur on Extreme Poverty and Human Rights." United Nations Human Rights Office of the High Commissioner. https://www.ohchr.org/EN/NewsEvents/Pages/DisplayNews.aspx?NewsID=22533.

REFERENCES

American Association for Public Opinion Research. 2020. "Questions to Ask When Writing About Polls." 2020. https://www.aapor.org/Education -Resources/For-Media/Questions-to-Ask-When-Writing-About-Polls .aspx.

American Psychiatric Association. 2013. *Diagnostic and Statistical Manual of Mental Disorders: DSM-5.* 5th Ed. Arlington, VA: American Psychiatric Association.

Amnesty International. 2020. "Death Penalty in 2019: Facts and Figures." April 21, 2020. https://www.amnesty.org/en/latest/news/2020/04/death-penalty-in -2019-facts-and-figures/.

Anderson, Carol. 2017. *White Rage: The Unspoken Truth of Our Racial Divide.* New York: Bloomsbury.

Annenberg Public Policy Center. 2014. "Americans Know Surprisingly Little About Their Government, Survey Finds." University of Pennsylvania. https://cdn.annenbergpublicpolicycenter.org/wp-content/uploads/2018/03 /Civics-survey-press-release-09-17-2014-for-PR-Newswire.pdf.

——. 2019. "Americans' Civics Knowledge Increases but Still Has a Long Way to Go." University of Pennsylvania. https://www.annenbergpublicpolicycenter .org/americans-civics-knowledge-increases-2019-survey/.

Ansolabehere, Stephen, John M. de Figueiredo, and James M. Snyder. 2003. "Why Is There So Little Money in U.S. Politics?" *Journal of Economic Perspectives* 17 (1): 105–30. https://doi.org/10.1257/089533003321164976.

Anson, Ian G., and Timothy Hellwig. 2015. "Economic Models of Voting." In *Emerging Trends in the Social and Behavioral Sciences*, ed. R. A. Scott and S. M. Kosslyn. New York: Wiley. https://https://onlinelibrary.wiley.com/doi/abs /10.1002/9781118900772.etrds0090.

Ariely, Dan. 2009. *Predictably Irrational: The Hidden Forces That Shape Our Decisions.* Rev. and expanded ed. New York: Harper Collins.

Azari, Julia. 2019a. "2019 Has Been Trump's Most Disjunctive Year Yet. And It's Only February." Vox. February 15, 2019. https://www.vox.com/mischiefs -of-faction/2019/2/15/18226485/trump-wall-shutdown-national -emergency.

——. 2019b. "It's the Institutions, Stupid: The Real Roots of America's Political Crisis." *Foreign Affairs* 98 (4): 10.

Bachman, Sara S., and Meg Comeau. 2010. "A Call to Action for Social Work: Minimizing Financial Hardship for Families of Children with Special Health Care Needs." *Health & Social Work* 35 (3): 233–38. https://doi .org/10.1093/hsw/35.3.233.

Bachrach, Peter, and Morton S. Baratz. 1962. "Two Faces of Power." *American Political Science Review* 56 (4): 947–52. https://doi.org/10.2307/1952796.

Ball, Annahita. 2020. "Calling Social Work to the Movement for Educational Justice." *Social Work Research*, December. https://doi.org/10.1093/swr/svaa014.

Ballotpedia. 2020a. "Independent Redistricting Commissions." Ballotpedia. 2020. https://ballotpedia.org/Independent_redistricting_commissions.

——. 2020b. "Judicial Election Methods by State." Ballotpedia. 2020. https://ballotpedia.org/Judicial_election_methods_by_state.

——. 2020c. "Supreme Court Cases, October Term 2019–2020." Ballotpedia. 2020. https://ballotpedia.org/Supreme_Court_cases,_October_term_2019-2020.

——. 2020d. "Election Results, 2020: Analysis of Rejected Ballots." Ballotpedia. December 23, 2020. https://ballotpedia.org/Election_results,_2020 :_Analysis_of_rejected_ballots.

Barber, Michael, and Jeremy C. Pope. 2019. "Does Party Trump Ideology? Disentangling Party and Ideology in America." *American Political Science Review* 113 (1): 38–54. https://doi.org/10.1017/S0003055418000795.

Barnes, Carolyn Y., and Julia R Henly. 2018. "'They Are Underpaid and Under-staffed': How Clients Interpret Encounters with Street-Level Bureaucrats." *Journal of Public Administration Research and Theory* 28 (2): 165–81. https://doi.org/10.1093/jopart/muy008.

Bartels, Larry M. 2014. "Ideology and Retrospection in Electoral Responses to the Great Recession." In *Mass Politics in Tough Times*, ed. Nancy Bermeo and Larry M. Bartels, 185–223. Oxford: Oxford University Press.

——. 2016. *Unequal Democracy: The Political Economy of the New Gilded Age.* New York: Russell Sage Foundation.

Baumgartner, Frank R., Jeffrey M. Berry, Marie Hojnacki, David C. Kimball, and Beth L. Leech. 2009. *Lobbying and Policy Change: Who Wins, Who Loses, and Why.* Chicago: University of Chicago Press.

Beard, Charles A. 1914. *An Economic Interpretation of the Constitution of the United States.* New York: MacMillan.

Béland, Daniel. 2007. *Social Security: History and Politics from the New Deal to the Privatization Debate.* Lawrence: University Press of Kansas.

Belluz, Julia. 2020. "We Finally Have a New US Maternal Mortality Estimate. It's Still Terrible." Vox. January 30, 2020. https://www.vox.com/2020 /1/30/21113782/pregnancy-deaths-us-maternal-mortality-rate.

Bent-Goodley, Tricia B., and June Gary Hopps. 2017. "Social Justice and Civil Rights: A Call to Action for Social Work." *Social Work* 62 (1): 5–8. https://doi.org/10.1093/sw/swwo81.

Berinsky, Adam J. 2002. "Silent Voices: Social Welfare Policy Opinions and Political Equality in America." *American Journal of Political Science* 46 (2): 276–87. https://doi.org/10.2307/3088376.

Bickel, Alexander M. 1986. *The Least Dangerous Branch: The Supreme Court at the Bar of Politics.* 2nd Ed. New Haven, CT: Yale University Press.

Binder, Sarah. 2015. "The Dysfunctional Congress." *Annual Review of Political Science* 18 (1): 85–101. https://doi.org/10.1146/annurev-polisci-110813 -032156.

Blattman, Chris, Michael Faye, Dean Karlan, Paul Niehaus, and Chris Udry. 2017. "Cash as Capital." *Stanford Social Innovation Review* 15 (3): 57–58.

Blendon, Robert J., and John M. Benson. 2001. "Americans' Views on Health Policy: A Fifty-Year Historical Perspective." *Health Affairs* 20 (2): 33–46. https://doi.org/10.1377/hlthaff.20.2.33.

Block, Fred. 1977. "The Ruling Class Does Not Rule: Notes on the Marxist Theory of the State." *Socialist Revolution* 33 (May–June). https://jacobinmag .com/2020/04/ruling-class-capitalist-state-reform-theory.

Block, Fred, and Frances Fox Piven. 2010. "Déjà Vu, All Over Again: A Comment on Jacob Hacker and Paul Pierson, 'Winner-Take-All Politics.'" *Politics & Society* 38 (2): 205–11. https://doi.org/10.1177/0032329210365043.

Bobo, Kimberley A., Jackie Kendall, and Steve Max. 2010. *Organizing for Social Change: Midwest Academy Manual for Activists.* 4th ed. Santa Ana, CA: Forum.

Bonica, Adam, Nolan McCarty, Keith T. Poole, and Howard Rosenthal. 2013. "Why Hasn't Democracy Slowed Rising Inequality?" *Journal of Economic Perspectives* 27 (3): 103–24. https://doi.org/10.1257/jep.27.3.103.

Bowman, Jarron. 2020. "Do the Affluent Override Average Americans? Measuring Policy Disagreement and Unequal Influence." *Social Science Quarterly* 101 (3): 1018–37. https://doi.org/10.1111/ssqu.12791.

Brennan Center for Justice. 2017. "Resources on Voter Fraud Claims." https://www.brennancenter.org/our-work/research-reports/resources -voter-fraud-claims.

——. 2019. "New Voting Restrictions in America." https://www.brennancenter .org/our-work/research-reports/new-voting-restrictions-america.

——. 2021. "State Voting Bills Tracker 2021." April 1, 2021. https://www .brennancenter.org/our-work/research-reports/state-voting-bills-tracker-2021.

Bright Line Watch. 2020. "Democracy in the COVID-19 Era: Bright Line Watch Expert Survey." http://brightlinewatch.org/bright-line-watch-august -2020-expert-survey/.

Bromfield, Nicole F., Meg Panichelli, and Moshoula Capous-Desyllas. 2021. "At the Intersection of COVID-19 and Sex Work in the United States: A Call for Social Work Action." *Affilia* 36 (2): 140–48. https://doi.org /10.1177/0886109920985131.

Broockman, David E., and Christopher Skovron. 2018. "Bias in Perceptions of Public Opinion Among Political Elites." *American Political Science Review* 112 (3): 542–63. https://doi.org/10.1017/S0003055418000011.

Brown, Garrett W., Iain McLean, and Alistair McMillan. 2018. "Duverger's Law." In *Oxford Dictionary of Politics and International Relations*. Oxford: Oxford University Press. https://www.oxfordreference.com/view/10.1093 /acref/9780199670840.001.0001/acref-9780199670840-e-382.

Brown, Nadia E., and Sarah Allen Gershon. 2016. *Distinct Identities: Minority Women in U.S. Politics*. New York: Routledge.

Bruch, Sarah K., Myra Marx Ferree, and Joe Soss. 2010. "From Policy to Polity: Democracy, Paternalism, and the Incorporation of Disadvantage." *American Sociological Review* 75 (2): 205–26. https://doi.org/10.1177/0003122410363563.

Bruch, Sarah K., and Joe Soss. 2018. "Schooling as a Formative Political Experience: Authority Relations and the Education of Citizens." *Perspectives on Politics* 16 (1): 36–57. https://doi.org/10.1017/S1537592717002195.

Bruenig, Matt. 2020. "What Exactly Is the Liberal Position on the Supreme Court?" *Jacobin*, September 21, 2020. https://jacobinmag.com/2020/09/liberal -supreme-court-rbg-ruth-bader-ginsburg.

Brunner, Eric, Stephen L. Ross, and Ebonya Washington. 2013. "Does Less Income Mean Less Representation?" *American Economic Journal: Economic Policy* 5 (2): 53–76. https://doi.org/10.2307/43189328.

Bump, Philip. 2018. "In About 20 Years, Half the Population Will Live in Eight States." *Washington Post*, July 12, 2018. https://www.washingtonpost .com/news/politics/wp/2018/07/12/in-about-20-years-half-the-population -will-live-in-eight-states/.

Butler, Daniel M., and David Nickerson. 2011. "Can Learning Constituency Opinion Affect How Legislators Vote? Results from a Field Experiment." *Quarterly Journal of Political Science* 6 (1): 55–83. https://doi.org/10.1561 /100.00011019.

Cai, Christopher, Jackson Runte, Isabel Ostrer, Kacey Berry, Ninez Ponce, Michael Rodriguez, Stefano Bertozzi, Justin S. White, and James G. Kahn. 2020. "Projected Costs of Single-Payer Healthcare Financing in the United States: A Systematic Review of Economic Analyses." *PLOS Medicine* 17 (1). https://doi.org/10.1371/journal.pmed.1003013.

REFERENCES

Calabresi, Steven G., and James Lindgren. 2006. "Term Limits for the Supreme Court: Life Tenure Reconsidered." *Harvard Journal of Law and Public Policy* 29 (3).

Campbell, Andrea Louise. 2011. *How Policies Make Citizens: Senior Political Activism and the American Welfare State.* Princeton, NJ: Princeton University Press.

Carnes, Nicholas. 2012. "Does the Numerical Underrepresentation of the Working Class in Congress Matter?: Class and Roll-Call Voting." *Legislative Studies Quarterly* 37 (1): 5–34. https://doi.org/10.1111/j.1939-9162.2011.00033.x.

——. 2013. *White-Collar Government: The Hidden Role of Class in Economic Policy Making.* Chicago: University of Chicago Press.

——. 2018. "Working-Class People Are Underrepresented in Politics. The Problem Isn't Voters." Vox. October 24, 2018. https://www.vox.com/policy-and-politics/2018/10/24/18009856/working-class-income-inequality-randy-bryce-alexandria-ocasio-cortez.

Carroll, Morgan. 2011. *Take Back Your Government: A Citizen's Guide to Grassroots Change.* Golden, CO: Fulcrum.

Case, Anne, and Angus Deaton. 2015. "Rising Morbidity and Mortality in Midlife Among White Non-Hispanic Americans in the 21st Century." *Proceedings of the National Academy of Sciences of the United States of America* 112 (49): 15078–83. https://doi.org/10.1073/pnas.1518393112.

——. 2017. "Mortality and Morbidity in the 21st Century." *Brookings Papers on Economic Activity* 2017: 397–476. https://doi.org/10.1353/eca.2017.0005.

Casillas, Christopher J., Peter K. Enns, and Patrick C. Wohlfarth. 2011. "How Public Opinion Constrains the U.S. Supreme Court." *American Journal of Political Science* 55 (1): 74–88. https://doi.org/10.1111/j.1540-5907.2010.00485.x.

Cassino, Daniel, and Peter Wooley. 2011. "Some News Leaves People Knowing Less." Poll. Fairleigh Dickinson University. http://publicmind.fdu.edu/2011/knowless/.

Cassino, Daniel, Peter Wooley, and Krista Jenkins. 2012. "What You Know Depends on What You Watch: Current Events Knowledge Across Popular News Sources." Poll. Fairleigh Dickinson University. http://publicmind.fdu.edu/2012/confirmed/.

Center for American Women and Politics. 2020. "Results: Women Candidates in the 2020 Elections." CAWP. November 4, 2020. https://cawp.rutgers.edu/election-analysis/results-women-candidates-2020-elections.

Center on Budget and Policy Priorities. 2019. "Policy Basics: Federal Tax Expenditures." https://www.cbpp.org/research/federal-tax/policy-basics-federal-tax-expenditures.

Centers for Disease Control. 2019. "Racial and Ethnic Disparities Continue in Pregnancy-Related Deaths." September 5, 2019. https://www.cdc.gov/media/releases/2019/p0905-racial-ethnic-disparities-pregnancy-deaths.html.

Centers for Medicare & Medicaid Services. 2020a. "National Health Expenditures Fact Sheet." March 24, 2020. https://www.cms.gov/Research-Statistics-Data-and-Systems/Statistics-Trends-and-Reports/NationalHealthExpendData/NHE-Fact-Sheet.

——. 2020b. "Health Insurance Exchanges 2020 Open Enrollment Report." April 1, 2020. https://www.cms.gov/files/document/4120-health-insurance-exchanges-2020-open-enrollment-report-final.pdf.

Cheek, Nathan N., and Eldar Shafir. 2020. "The Thick Skin Bias in Judgments About People in Poverty." *Behavioural Public Policy*, August, 1–26. https://doi.org/10.1017/bpp.2020.33.

Chenoweth, Erica, and Jeremy Pressman. 2020. "This Summer's Black Lives Matter Protesters Were Overwhelmingly Peaceful, Our Research Finds." *Washington Post*, October 16, 2020. https://www.washingtonpost.com/politics/2020/10/16/this-summers-black-lives-matter-protesters-were-overwhelming-peaceful-our-research-finds/.

Chermak, Steven M., Joshua D. Freilich, and Michael Suttmoeller. 2011. "The Organizational Dynamics of Far-Right Hate Groups in the United States: Comparing Violent to Non-Violent Organizations." National Consortium for the Study of Terrorism and Responses to Terrorism. https://www.dhs.gov/sites/default/files/publications/944_OPSR_TEVUS_Comparing-Violent-Nonviolent-Far-Right-Hate-Groups_Dec2011-508.pdf.

Chinoy, Sahil. 2019. "What Happened to America's Political Center of Gravity?" *New York Times*, June 26, 2019. https://www.nytimes.com/interactive/2019/06/26/opinion/sunday/republican-platform-far-right.html.

Christensen, Julian, and Donald P. Moynihan. 2020. "Motivated Reasoning and Policy Information: Politicians Are More Resistant to Debiasing Interventions Than the General Public." *Behavioural Public Policy*, November. https://doi.org/10.1017/bpp.2020.50.

Churchill, Ward. 2008. "The Pinkerton Detective Agency: Prefiguring the FBI." In *Race and Human Rights*, ed. Curtis Stokes, 53–118. East Lansing: Michigan State University Press.

REFERENCES

CNN. 2016. "2016 Election Results: Exit Polls." November 23, 2016. http://2016 .elections.cnn.com/election/2016/results/exit-polls.

Cohen, Michael D., James G. March, and Johan P. Olsen. 1972. "A Garbage Can Model of Organizational Choice." *Administrative Science Quarterly* 17 (1): 1–25. https://doi.org/10.2307/2392088.

Congressional Research Service. 2020. "Membership of the 116th Congress: A Profile." https://fas.org/sgp/crs/misc/R45583.pdf.

Converse, Philip E. 1964. "The Nature of Belief Systems in Mass Publics." In *Ideology and Discontent*, ed. David E. Apter. Glencoe, IL: Free Press.

Cooper, David, Elise Gould, and Ben Zipperer. 2019. "Low-Wage Workers Are Suffering from a Decline in the Real Value of the Federal Minimum Wage." Economic Policy Institute. https://www.epi.org/publication/labor-day-2019 -minimum-wage/#:~:text=The%20federal%20minimum%20wage%20 is,hour%20in%20this%20year's%20dollars.

Coppock, Alexander, Emily Ekins, and David Kirby. 2018. "The Long-Lasting Effects of Newspaper Op-Eds on Public Opinion." *Quarterly Journal of Political Science* 13 (1): 59–87. https://doi.org/10.1561/100.00016112.

Corak, Miles. 2016. "Inequality from Generation to Generation: The United States in Comparison." Discussion Paper No. 9929. Institute for the Study of Labor. http://ftp.iza.org/dp9929.pdf.

Cordova, Gennette. 2020. "Black Progress Has Always Been Met with Racist Backlash." *Teen Vogue*, July 31, 2020. https://www.teenvogue.com/story/white -backlash-black-progress.

Coryn, Chris L. S., Lindsay A. Noakes, Carl D. Westine, and Daniela C. Schröter. 2011. "A Systematic Review of Theory-Driven Evaluation Practice from 1990 to 2009." *American Journal of Evaluation* 32 (2): 199–226. https:// doi.org/10.1177/1098214010389321.

Council on Social Work Education. 2015. "Educational Policy and Accreditation Standards."

Crabtree-Nelson, Sonya, Susan F. Grossman, and Marta Lundy. 2016. "A Call to Action: Domestic Violence Education in Social Work." *Social Work* 61 (4): 359–62. https://doi.org/10.1093/sw/sww050.

Craig, Maureen A., and Jennifer A. Richeson. 2017. "Information About the US Racial Demographic Shift Triggers Concerns About Anti-White Discrimination Among the Prospective White 'Minority.'" *PLoS ONE* 12 (9): e0185389. https://doi.org/10.1371/journal.pone.0185389.

Cummins, Linda K., Katharine V. Byers, and Laura E. Pedrick. 2011. *Policy Practice for Social Workers: New Strategies for a New Era.* Updated ed. Boston: Allyn and Bacon.

Dahl, Robert Alan. 2003. *How Democratic Is the American Constitution?* 2nd ed. The Castle Lectures in Ethics, Politics and Economics. New Haven, CT: Yale University Press.

——. 2005. *Who Governs? Democracy and Power in an American City.* 2nd ed. New Haven, CT: Yale University Press.

Dalal, Farhad. 2018. *CBT: The Cognitive Behavioural Tsunami: Managerialism, Politics, and the Corruptions of Science.* New York: Routledge.

Davis, Angela M. 2013. "Transcription: Angela Davis 'Freedom Is a Constant Struggle: Closures and Continuities."*Critical Legal Thinking* (blog). November 25, 2013. https://criticallegalthinking.com/2013/11/25/transcription-angela-davis -freedom-constant-struggle-closures-continuities/.

Dawood, Yasmin. 2015. "Campaign Finance and American Democracy." *Annual Review of Political Science* 18 (1): 329–48. https://doi.org/10.1146/annurev -polisci-010814-104523.

Day, Meagan, and Micah Uetricht. 2020. *Bigger Than Bernie: How We Go from the Sanders Campaign to Democratic Socialism.* London: Verso.

Delli Carpini, Michael X., and Scott Keeter. 1996. *What Americans Know About Politics and Why It Matters.* New Haven, CT: Yale University Press.

Democracy Forward. 2020. "Democracy Forward Sues Trump Administration for Communications with Fox News, OANN During COVID-19 Response." Press release. June 23, 2020. https://democracyforward.org/press/df-sues-trump -admin-for-communications-with-foxnews-oann-during-covid-19-response/.

DeParle, Jason. 2020. "Vast Federal Aid Has Capped Rise in Poverty, Studies Find." *New York Times,* June 21, 2020. https://www.nytimes.com/2020/06/21 /us/politics/coronavirus-poverty.html.

DeSilver, Drew. 2018a. "Congress Has Long Struggled to Pass Spending Bills on Time." Pew Research Center. https://www.pewresearch.org/fact-tank/2018 /01/16/congress-has-long-struggled-to-pass-spending-bills-on-time/.

——. 2018b. "U.S. Voter Turnout Trails Most Developed Countries." Pew Research Center. https://www.pewresearch.org/fact-tank/2018/05/21/u-s-voter-turnout -trails-most-developed-countries/.

——. 2018c. "For Most Americans, Real Wages Have Barely Budged for Decades." Pew Research Center. https://www.pewresearch.org/fact-tank/2018/08/07 /for-most-us-workers-real-wages-have-barely-budged-for-decades/.

Dews, Fred. 2017. "A Primer on Gerrymandering and Political Polarization." *Brookings* (blog). July 6, 2017. https://www.brookings.edu/blog/brookings -now/2017/07/06/a-primer-on-gerrymandering-and-political-polarization/.

DiJulio, Bianca, Jamie Firth, and Mollyann Brodie. 2015. "Data Note: Americans' Views on the U.S. Role in Global Health." Kaiser Family Foundation. https://www.kff.org/global-health-policy/poll-finding/data-note-americans -views-on-the-u-s-role-in-global-health/.

Dillon, Lindsey, Christopher Sellers, Vivian Underhill, Nicholas Shapiro, Jennifer Liss Ohayon, Marianne Sullivan, Phil Brown, Jill Harrison, and Sara Wylie. 2018. "The Environmental Protection Agency in the Early Trump Administration: Prelude to Regulatory Capture." *American Journal of Public Health* 108 (S2): S89–94. https://doi.org/10.2105/AJPH.2018.304360.

Domanski, M. D. 1998. "Prototypes of Social Work Political Participation: An Empirical Model." *Social Work* 43 (2): 156–67. https://doi.org/10.1093/sw /43.2.156.

Domhoff, G. William. (1956) 2007. "C. Wright Mills, Power Structure Research, and the Failures of Mainstream Political Science." *New Political Science* 29 (1): 97–114. https://doi.org/10.1080/07393140601170867.

——. 2014. *Who Rules America? The Triumph of the Corporate Rich.* 7th ed. New York: McGraw-Hill Education.

Donnelly, Kevin P., and David A. Rochefort. 2012. "The Lessons of 'Lesson Drawing': How the Obama Administration Attempted to Learn from Failure of the Clinton Health Plan." *Journal of Policy History* 24 (2): 184–223. https://doi.org/10.1017/S0898030612000024.

Douglass, Frederick. 1857. "Speech on West India Emancipation." August 3, 1857. https://rbscp.lib.rochester.edu/4398.

Dowling, Conor M., Michael Henderson, and Michael G. Miller. 2020. "Knowledge Persists, Opinions Drift: Learning and Opinion Change in a Three-Wave Panel Experiment." *American Politics Research* 48 (2): 263–74. https://doi.org/10.1177/1532673X19832543.

Downey, Kirstin. 2009. *The Woman Behind the New Deal: The Life of Frances Perkins, FDR's Secretary of Labor and His Moral Conscience.* New York: Nan A. Talese.

Drezner, Daniel W. 2020. *The Toddler in Chief: What Donald Trump Teaches Us About the Modern Presidency.* Chicago: University of Chicago Press.

Drutman, Lee. 2015. "Will 'Decoherence' Be the Doom of American Democracy?" Vox. September 11, 2015. https://www.vox.com/polyarchy/2015/9/11/9310873 /decoherence-democracy-doomed.

———. 2017. "'Conservative' Means Different Things to Different Conservatives." *Pacific Standard*, May 3, 2017. https://psmag.com/news/america-not-as-politically-conservative-as-you-think-26845.

———. 2019. "The Moderate Middle Is a Myth." *FiveThirtyEight* (blog). September 24, 2019. https://fivethirtyeight.com/features/the-moderate-middle-is-a-myth/.

Dutta-Gupta, Indivar. 2011. "Taking Stock of the Safety Net, Part 6: It Works, But It Doesn't Do Enough." Center on Budget and Policy Priorities. December 21, 2011. https://www.cbpp.org/blog/taking-stock-of-the-safety-net-part-6-it-works-but-it-doesnt-do-enough.

Eckman, Sarah J. 2019. "Apportionment and Redistricting Process for the U.S. House of Representatives." Congressional Research Service. https://fas.org/sgp/crs/misc/R45951.pdf.

Economic Policy Institute. 2020. "Minimum Wage Tracker." *Economic Policy Institute* (blog). November 5, 2020. https://www.epi.org/minimum-wage-tracker/

Eddington, Sean M. 2018. "The Communicative Constitution of Hate Organizations Online: A Semantic Network Analysis of 'Make America Great Again.'" *Social Media + Society* 4 (3). https://doi.org/10.1177/2056305118790763.

Edwards, Ashley N. 2014. "Dynamics of Economic Well-Being: Poverty, 2009–2011." U.S. Census Bureau. https://www.census.gov/prod/2014pubs/p70-137.pdf.

Ehrenreich, John. 2014. *The Altruistic Imagination: A History of Social Work and Social Policy in the United States.* Ithaca, NY: Cornell University Press.

Engstrom, Richard L. 2020. "Introduction to the Mini Symposium on Partisan Gerrymandering." *Social Science Quarterly* 101 (1): 8–9. https://doi.org/10.1111/ssqu.12744.

Equal Justice Initiative. 2017. "Lynching in America: Confronting the Legacy of Racial Terror, Third Edition." https://eji.org/wp-content/uploads/2020/09/lynching-in-america-3d-ed-091620.pdf.

Erikson, Robert S. 2015. "Income Inequality and Policy Responsiveness." *Annual Review of Political Science* 18 (1): 11–29. https://doi.org/10.1146/annurev-polisci-020614-094706.

Ernst, Rose, Linda Nguyen, and Kamilah C. Taylor. 2013. "Citizen Control: Race at the Welfare Office." *Social Science Quarterly* 94 (5): 1283–1307. https://doi.org/10.1111/ssqu.12013.

Esping-Andersen, Gøsta. 1990. *The Three Worlds of Welfare Capitalism.* Princeton, NJ: Princeton University Press.

REFERENCES

Espírito-Santo, Ana, André Freire, and Sofia Serra-Silva. 2020. "Does Women's Descriptive Representation Matter for Policy Preferences? The Role of Political Parties." *Party Politics* 26 (2): 227–37. https://doi.org/10.1177/1354068818764011.

Ettlinger, Michael, and Jordan Hensley. 2020. "The 2021 Senate Will Be Unrepresentative." November 12, 2020. https://medium.com/@mettlinger/the-2021-senate-will-be-unrepresentative-8a6ee7dbfb08.

Evermore, Michele. 2019. "Are State Unemployment Systems Still Able to Counter Recessions?" National Employment Law Project. https://www.nelp.org/publication/state-unemployment-systems-still-able-counter-recessions/.

Evers-Hilstrom, Karl. 2020. "Majority of Lawmakers in 116th Congress Are Millionaires." OpenSecrets News. April 23, 2020. https://www.opensecrets.org/news/2020/04/majority-of-lawmakers-millionaires/.

Ezell, Mark. 1993. "The Political Activity of Social Workers: A Post-Reagan Update." *Journal of Sociology & Social Welfare* 20 (4), article 6.

Faricy, Christopher. 2016. *Welfare for the Wealthy: Parties, Social Spending, and Inequality in the US.* New York: Cambridge University Press.

Farmelo, Martha. 2015. "Suggested Guidelines for Creating a Theory of Change." https://nonprofitbuilder.org/storage/335/Suggested-Guidelines-for-Creating-a-Theory-of-Change-Martha-Farmelo.pdf.

FBI Counterterrorism Division. 2006. "White Supremacist Infiltration of Law Enforcement." http://s3.documentcloud.org/documents/402521/doc-26-white-supremacist-infiltration.pdf.

Fenno, Richard F. 2003. *Home Style: House Members in Their Districts.* New York: Longman.

Ferejohn, John E. 2002. "Constitutional Review in the Global Context Legislatures, Courts, and the Contestability of Rights: A Conversation." *New York University Journal of Legislation and Public Policy* 6 (1): 49–60.

Fessler, Pam, and Elena Moore. 2020. "More Than 550,000 Primary Absentee Ballots Rejected in 2020, Far Outpacing 2016." NPR. August 22, 2020. https://www.npr.org/2020/08/22/904693468/more-than-550-000-primary-absentee-ballots-rejected-in-2020-far-outpacing-2016.

Figueira-McDonough, Josefina. 1993. "Policy Practice: The Neglected Side of Social Work Intervention." *Social Work*, March. https://doi.org/10.1093/sw/38.2.179.

File, Thom. 2017. "Voting in America: A Look at the 2016 Presidential Election." U.S. Census Bureau. https://www.census.gov/newsroom/blogs/random-samplings/2017/05/voting_in_america.html.

Finkel, Eli J., Christopher A. Bail, Mina Cikara, Peter H. Ditto, Shanto Iyengar, Samara Klar, Lilliana Mason, et al. 2020. "Political Sectarianism in America." *Science* 370 (6516): 533–36. https://doi.org/10.1126/science.abe1715.

Fiorina, Morris P. 2017. *Unstable Majorities: Polarization, Party Sorting, and Political Stalemate.* Stanford, CA: Hoover Institution Press.

Fiorina, Morris P., Samuel J. Abrams, and Jeremy Pope. 2011. *Culture War? The Myth of a Polarized America.* 3rd ed. Great Questions in Politics. Boston: Longman.

Fishkin, Joseph, and David E. Pozen. 2018. "Asymmetric Constitutional Hardball." *Columbia Law Review* 118 (3): 915–82.

Flores, Andrew, Charles Gossett, Gabriele Magni, and Andrew Reynolds. 2020. "11 Openly LGBTQ Lawmakers Will Take Their Seats in the Next Congress. That's a Record in Both Numbers and Diversity." *Washington Post,* November 30, 2020. https://www.washingtonpost.com/politics/2020/11/30/11-lgbtq-legislators-will-take-their-seats-next-congress-largest-most-diverse-group-ever/.

Floyd, Ife. 2020. "Cash Assistance Should Reach Millions More Families." Center on Budget and Policy Priorities. https://www.cbpp.org/research/family-income-support/cash-assistance-should-reach-millions-more-families.

Foa, R. S., A. Klassen, M. Slade, A. Rand, and R. Collins. 2020. "Global Satisfaction with Democracy Report 2020." Centre for the Future of Democracy. https://www.bennettinstitute.cam.ac.uk/media/uploads/files/DemocracyReport2020.pdf.

Foner, Eric. 1993. *Freedom's Lawmakers: A Directory of Black Officeholders During Reconstruction.* New York: Oxford University Press.

Fowler, Anthony, and Andrew B. Hall. 2018. "Do Shark Attacks Influence Presidential Elections? Reassessing a Prominent Finding on Voter Competence." *Journal of Politics* 80 (4): 1423–37. https://doi.org/10.1086/699244.

Fox, Cybelle. 2012. *Three Worlds of Relief: Race, Immigration, and the American Welfare State from the Progressive Era to the New Deal.* Princeton, NJ: Princeton University Press.

Fox, Liana. 2020. "The Supplemental Poverty Measure: 2019." https://www.census.gov/library/publications/2020/demo/p60-272.html.

Funiciello, Theresa. 1993. *Tyranny of Kindness: Dismantling the Welfare System to End Poverty in America.* New York: Atlantic Monthly Press. https://archive.org/details/tyrannyofkindnesoother.

Gallup. 2007. "Healthcare System." June 26, 2007. https://news.gallup.com/poll/4708/Healthcare-System.aspx.

———. 2019. "Confidence in Institutions." https://news.gallup.com/poll/1597 /confidence-institutions.aspx.

Galvin, Daniel J., and Jacob S. Hacker. 2020. "The Political Effects of Policy Drift: Policy Stalemate and American Political Development." *Studies in American Political Development* 34 (2): 216–38. https://doi.org/10.1017 /S0898588X2000005X.

Gans, Herbert J. 1971. "The Uses of Poverty: The Poor Pay All." *Social Policy*, July/August, 20–24.

———. 1972. "The Positive Functions of Poverty." *American Journal of Sociology* 78 (2): 275–89. https://doi.org/10.1086/225324.

Ganzach, Yoav, and Yaacov Schul. 2020. "Partisan Ideological Attitudes: Liberals Are Tolerant; the Intelligent Are Intolerant." *Journal of Personality and Social Psychology*. Advance online publication. https://doi.org/10.1037/pspi0000324.

Garcia, Emma. 2020. "Schools Are Still Segregated, and Black Children Are Paying a Price." Economic Policy Institute. https://www.epi.org/publication /schools-are-still-segregated-and-black-children-are-paying-a-price/.

Gause, LaGina. 2020. "Revealing Issue Salience Via Costly Protest: How Legislative Behavior Following Protest Advantages Low-Resource Groups." *British Journal of Political Science*, 1–21. https://doi.org/10.1017/S0007123420000423.

Geiger, A. W. 2019. "In 116th Congress, At Least 13 Percent of Lawmakers Are Immigrants or the Children of Immigrants." *Pew Research Center* (blog). January 24, 2019. https://www.pewresearch.org/fact-tank/2019/01/24/in-116th -congress-at-least-13-of-lawmakers-are-immigrants-or-the-children-of -immigrants/.

Gilens, Martin. 1999. *Why Americans Hate Welfare: Race, Media, and the Politics of Antipoverty Policy*. Chicago: University of Chicago Press.

———. 2012. *Affluence and Influence: Economic Inequality and Political Power in America*. Princeton, NJ: Princeton University Press.

Gilens, Martin, and Benjamin I. Page. 2014. "Testing Theories of American Politics: Elites, Interest Groups, and Average Citizens." *Perspectives on Politics* 12 (3): 564–81. https://doi.org/10.1017/S1537592714001595.

Gillmor, Dan. 2006. *We the Media: Grassroots Journalism by the People, for the People*. Sebastopol, CA: O'Reilly.

Giridharadas, Anand. 2019. *Winners Take All: The Elite Charade of Changing the World*. New York: Vintage.

Golde, Calvis. 2020. "Experts Tout Proposals for Supreme Court Term Limits." *SCOTUSblog* (blog). August 4, 2020. https://www.scotusblog.com/2020 /08/experts-tout-proposals-for-supreme-court-term-limits/.

Gould, Elise, and Hilary Wething. 2012. "U.S. Poverty Rates Higher, Safety Net Weaker Than in Peer Countries." Economic Policy Institute. https://www.epi.org/publication/ib339-us-poverty-higher-safety-net-weaker/.

GovTrack. 2018. "With Kavanaugh Vote, the Senate Reaches a Historic Low in Democratic Metric." October 7, 2018. https://govtrackinsider.com/with-kavanaugh-vote-the-senate-reaches-a-historic-low-in-democratic-metric-dfbof5fa7fa.

——. 2021. "Statistics and Historical Comparison." https://www.govtrack.us/congress/bills/statistics.

Green, Donald P., Mary C. McGrath, and Peter M. Aronow. 2013. "Field Experiments and the Study of Voter Turnout." *Journal of Elections, Public Opinion and Parties* 23 (1): 27–48. https://doi.org/10.1080/17457289.2012.728223.

Green, Mike, Henry Moore, John O'Brien, and John L. McKnight. 2006. *When People Care Enough to Act: ABCD in Action.* Toronto: Inclusion.

Grieco, Elizabeth. 2020. "U.S. Newspapers Have Shed Half of Their Newsroom Employees Since 2008." Pew Research Center. https://www.pewresearch.org/fact-tank/2020/04/20/u-s-newsroom-employment-has-dropped-by-a-quarter-since-2008/.

Griffin, John D., and Claudia Anewalt-Remsburg. 2013. "Legislator Wealth and the Effort to Repeal the Estate Tax." *American Politics Research* 41 (4): 599–622. https://doi.org/10.1177/1532673X12472363.

Groenendyk, Eric, and Yanna Krupnikov. 2020. "What Motivates Reasoning? A Theory of Goal-Dependent Political Evaluation." *American Journal of Political Science.* https://doi.org/10.1111/ajps.12562.

Grossmann, Matt, and David A. Hopkins. 2016. *Asymmetric Politics: Ideological Republicans and Group Interest Democrats.* Oxford: Oxford University Press.

Grote, Rainer. 2016. "Parliamentary Systems." In *Max Planck Encyclopedia of Comparative Constitutional Law.* Oxford: Oxford University Press. https://doi.org/10.1093/law-mpeccol/e410.013.410.

Gupta, Sujata. 2020. "How Next-Gen Computer Generated Maps Detect Partisan Gerrymandering." *Science News* (blog). September 7, 2020. https://www.sciencenews.org/article/gerrymandering-elections-next-gen-computer-generated-maps.

Guzman, Gloria G. 2019. "Household Income: 2018." U.S. Census Bureau. https://www.census.gov/library/publications/2019/acs/acsbr18-01.html.

Hacker, Jacob S. 2002. *The Divided Welfare State: The Battle Over Public and Private Social Benefits in the United States.* New York: Cambridge University Press.

——. 2005. "Policy Drift: The Hidden Politics of US Welfare State Retrenchment." In *Beyond Continuity: Institutional Change in Advanced Political Economies*, ed. Kathleen Thelen and Wolfgang Streeck, 40–82. Oxford: Oxford University Press.

——. 2010. "The Road to Somewhere: Why Health Reform Happened: Or Why Political Scientists Who Write About Public Policy Shouldn't Assume They Know How to Shape It." *Perspectives on Politics* 8 (3): 861–76. https://doi.org/10.1017/S1537592710002021.

Hacker, Jacob S., and Paul Pierson. 2010. *Winner-Take-All Politics: How Washington Made the Rich Richer—and Turned Its Back on the Middle Class*. New York: Simon & Schuster.

——. 2014. "After the 'Master Theory': Downs, Schattschneider, and the Rebirth of Policy-Focused Analysis." *Perspectives on Politics* 12 (3): 643–62. https://doi.org/10.1017/S1537592714001637.

——. 2020. *Let Them Eat Tweets: How the Right Rules in an Age of Extreme Inequality*. New York: Liveright.

Hamilton, Alexander, James Madison, and John Jay. (1788) 1992. *The Federalist Papers*. Cutchogue, NY: Buccaneer.

Han, Hahrie. 2020. "Problems of Power." *Stanford Social Innovation Review*, Winter.

Han, Jeehoon, Bruce Meyer, and James Sullivan. 2020. "Income and Poverty in the COVID-19 Pandemic." Cambridge, MA: National Bureau of Economic Research. https://doi.org/10.3386/w27729.

Hasen, Richard L. 2020. "Bring On the 28th Amendment." *New York Times*, June 29, 2020. https://www.nytimes.com/2020/06/29/opinion/sunday/voting-rights.html.

Hasenfeld, Yeheskel. 2000. "Organizational Forms as Moral Practices: The Case of Welfare Departments." *Social Service Review* 74 (3): 329–51. https://doi.org/10.1086/516408.

Helliwell, John F., Richard Layard, Jeffrey Sachs, and Jan-Emmanuel De Neve, eds. 2020. "World Happiness Report 2020." New York: Sustainable Development Solutions Network. https://worldhappiness.report/ed/2020/#read.

Hendrickson, Clara. 2019. "Local Journalism in Crisis: Why America Must Revive Its Local Newsrooms." Brookings. https://www.brookings.edu/research/local-journalism-in-crisis-why-america-must-revive-its-local-newsrooms/.

Herd, Pamela, and Donald P. Moynihan. 2018. *Administrative Burden: Policymaking by Other Means*. New York: Russell Sage Foundation.

Herman, Edward S., and Noam Chomsky. 2002. *Manufacturing Consent: The Political Economy of the Mass Media*. New York: Pantheon.

REFERENCES

Hernes, Helga Maria. 1987. *Welfare State and Woman Power: Essays in State Feminism*. Oslo: Norwegian University Press.

Hersh, Eitan. 2020. *Politics Is for Power: How to Move Beyond Political Hobbyism, Take Action, and Make Real Change*. New York: Scribner.

Hertel-Fernandez, Alexander. 2020. "How Policymakers Can Craft Measures That Endure and Build Political Power." Roosevelt Institute. https://roosevelt institute.org/publications/how-policymakers-can-craft-measures-that -endure-and-build-political-power/.

Hertel-Fernandez, Alexander, and Carlos Guillermo Smith. 2020. "Revitalizing People-Based Government." *Stanford Social Innovation Review*, Winter.

Hibbing, John R., and Elizabeth Theiss-Morse. 2002. *Stealth Democracy: Americans' Beliefs About How Government Should Work*. Cambridge: Cambridge University Press.

Hipple, Liz. 2019. "Low Intergenerational Mobility in the United States Shows Impact of Race and Public Policy." *Equitable Growth* (blog). May 30, 2019. http://www.equitablegrowth.org/low-intergenerational-mobility -in-the-united-states-shows-impact-of-race-and-public-policy/.

Ho, D. E., and K. M. Quinn. 2010. "Did a Switch in Time Save Nine?" *Journal of Legal Analysis* 2 (1): 69–113. https://doi.org/10.1093/jla/2.1.69.

Hoefer, Richard. 2019. *Advocacy Practice for Social Justice*. 4th ed. New York: Oxford University Press.

Hoffman, Lindsay H. 2019. "Political Knowledge and Communication." In *Oxford Research Encyclopedia of Communication*, ed. Jon F. Nussbaum. Oxford: Oxford University Press. https://doi.org/10.1093/acrefore /9780190228613.013.109.

Holt, Kristoffer. 2019. *Right-Wing Alternative Media*. New York: Routledge.

Horowitz, Juliana Menasce, Ruth Igielnik, and Rakesh Kochhar. 2020. "Trends in U.S. Income and Wealth Inequality." *Pew Research Center's Social & Demographic Trends Project* (blog). January 9, 2020. https://www.pewsocialtrends .org/2020/01/09/trends-in-income-and-wealth-inequality/.

Howard, Christopher. 1997. *The Hidden Welfare State: Tax Expenditures and Social Policy in the United States*. Princeton, NJ: Princeton University Press.

Howard, Christopher, Amirio Freeman, April Wilson, and Eboni Brown. 2017. "The Polls—Trends: Poverty." *Public Opinion Quarterly* 81 (3): 769–89. https://doi.org/10.1093/poq/nfx022.

Huang, Jon, Samuel Jacoby, Michael Strickland, and K. K. Rebecca Lai. 2016. "Election 2016: Exit Polls." *New York Times*, November 8, 2016. https://

www.nytimes.com/interactive/2016/11/08/us/politics/election-exit-polls
.html.

Hughey, Matthew W. 2014. "White Backlash in the 'Post-Racial' United States."
Ethnic and Racial Studies 37 (5): 721–30. https://doi.org/10.1080/01419870
.2014.886710.

Illing, Sean. 2019. "How Fox News Evolved Into a Propaganda Operation." Vox.
March 22, 2019. https://www.vox.com/2019/3/22/18275835/fox-news-trump
-propaganda-tom-rosenstiel.

——. 2020. "Trump's War on Fox News and the Future of Right-Wing Media."
Vox. November 13, 2020. https://www.vox.com/policy-and-politics/21557244
/2020-election-fox-news-newsmax-oan-brian-stelter.

Ingraham, Christopher. 2020a. "The United States Is Backsliding Into Autocracy
Under Trump, Scholars Warn." *Washington Post*, September 18, 2020. https://
www.washingtonpost.com/business/2020/09/18/united-states-is-backsliding
-into-autocracy-under-trump-scholars-warn/.

——. 2020b. "GOP Leaders' Embrace of Trump's Refusal to Concede Fits Pattern of Rising Authoritarianism, Data Shows." *Washington Post*, November 12,
2020. https://www.washingtonpost.com/business/2020/11/12/republican-party
-trump-authoritarian-data/.

International Council for Diplomacy and Dialogue. 2020. "Race, Class, Resistance: Francis Fox Piven in Conversation with Stephen Bronner." *The Crisis*.
https://www.youtube.com/watch?v=gGnOr9hLOeM.

Iyengar, Shanto, Yphtach Lelkes, Matthew Levendusky, Neil Malhotra, and
Sean J. Westwood. 2019. "The Origins and Consequences of Affective
Polarization in the United States." *Annual Review of Political Science* 22 (1):
129–46. https://doi.org/10.1146/annurev-polisci-051117-073034.

Jacobs, Lawrence R., and Robert Y. Shapiro. 2000. *Politicians Don't Pander:
Political Manipulation and the Loss of Democratic Responsiveness*. Chicago:
University of Chicago Press.

Jacobson, W. B. 2001. "Beyond Therapy: Bringing Social Work Back to Human
Services Reform." *Social Work* 46 (1): 51–61. https://doi.org/10.1093/sw
/46.1.51.

Jennings, Julie, and Jared C. Nagel. 2019. "Federal Workforce Statistics Sources:
OPM and OMB." Congressional Research Service. https://fas.org/sgp/crs
/misc/R43590.pdf.

Joint Committee on Taxation. 2019. "Estimates of Federal Tax Expenditures
for Fiscal Years 2019–2023." JCX-55-19. Congress of the United States.
https://www.jct.gov/publications.html?func=startdown&id=5238.

Jones, Bradley. 2018. "Most Americans Want to Limit Campaign Spending, Say Big Donors Have Greater Political Influence." Pew Research Center. https://www.pewresearch.org/fact-tank/2018/05/08/most-americans -want-to-limit-campaign-spending-say-big-donors-have-greater-political -influence/.

Jurkowitz, Mark, Amy Mitchell, Elisa Shearer, and Mason Walker. 2020. "U.S. Media Polarization and the 2020 Election: A Nation Divided." *Pew Research Center's Journalism Project* (blog). January 24, 2020. https://www .journalism.org/2020/01/24/u-s-media-polarization-and-the-2020-election -a-nation-divided/.

Kalla, Joshua L., and David E. Broockman. 2018. "The Minimal Persuasive Effects of Campaign Contact in General Elections: Evidence from 49 Field Experiments." *American Political Science Review* 112 (1): 148–66. https://doi.org/10.1017/S0003055417000363.

——. 2020. "Reducing Exclusionary Attitudes Through Interpersonal Conversation: Evidence from Three Field Experiments." *American Political Science Review* 114 (2): 410–25. https://doi.org/10.1017/S0003055419000923.

Kaba, Mariame. 2021. *We Do This 'Til We Free Us: Abolitionist Organizing and Transforming Justice.* Chicago: Haymarket.

Kaplan, Jonas T., Sarah I. Gimbel, and Sam Harris. 2016. "Neural Correlates of Maintaining One's Political Beliefs in the Face of Counterevidence." *Scientific Reports* 6 (1): 39589. https://doi.org/10.1038/srep39589.

Kasmir, Sharryn. 2018. "Precarity." *Cambridge Encyclopedia of Anthropology*, March. https://www.anthroencyclopedia.com/entry/precarity.

Katznelson, Ira. 2006. *When Affirmative Action Was White: An Untold History of Racial Inequality in Twentieth-Century America.* New York: Norton.

Kessler, Ronald C., Patricia Berglund, Olga Demler, Robert Jin, Kathleen R. Merikangas, and Ellen E. Walters. 2005. "Lifetime Prevalence and Age-of-Onset Distributions of DSM-IV Disorders in the National Comorbidity Survey Replication." *Archives of General Psychiatry* 62 (6): 593–602. https:// doi.org/10.1001/archpsyc.62.6.593.

Keyssar, Alexander. 2009. *The Right to Vote: The Contested History of Democracy in the United States.* Rev. ed. New York: Basic Books.

——. 2012. "Voter Suppression Returns." *Harvard Magazine,* June 15, 2012. https://harvardmagazine.com/2012/07/voter-suppression-returns.

Kiel, Paul. 2020. "Has the IRS Hit Bottom?" ProPublica. June 30, 2020. https://www.propublica.org/article/has-the-irs-hit-bottom?token=PNdp3 JnBZi8MNvZOwQA12CU3X1KFZTkE.

Kiel, Paul, and Hannah Fresques. 2019. "Where in the U.S. Are You Most Likely to Be Audited by the IRS?" ProPublica. https://projects.propublica. org/graphics/eitc-audit.

Kim, Saeromi, and Esteban Cardemil. 2012. "Effective Psychotherapy with Low-Income Clients: The Importance of Attending to Social Class." *Journal of Contemporary Psychotherapy* 42 (1): 27–35. https://doi.org/10.1007/s10879 -011-9194-0.

King, Martin Luther, Jr. 1963. "Letter from a Birmingham Jail." https://www .africa.upenn.edu/Articles_Gen/Letter_Birmingham.html.

Kingdon, John W. 2011. *Agendas, Alternatives, and Public Policies.* Updated 2nd ed. Longman Classics in Political Science. Boston: Longman.

Klein, Ezra. 2014. "The Green Lantern Theory of the Presidency, Explained." *Vox* (blog). May 20, 2014. https://www.vox.com/2014/5/20/5732208/the-green -lantern-theory-of-the-presidency-explained.

Klein, Naomi. 2007. *The Shock Doctrine: The Rise of Disaster Capitalism.* New York: Metropolitan.

Koerth, Maggie. 2019. "Everyone Knows Money Influences Politics . . . Except Scientists." *FiveThirtyEight* (blog). June 4, 2019. https://fivethirtyeight.com /features/everyone-knows-money-influences-politics-except-scientists/.

Koerth, Maggie, and Amelia Thomson-DeVeaux. 2020. "Many Americans Are Convinced Crime Is Rising in the U.S. They're Wrong." *FiveThirtyEight* (blog). August 3, 2020. https://fivethirtyeight.com/features/many-americans -are-convinced-crime-is-rising-in-the-u-s-theyre-wrong/.

Kraus, Michael W., and Bennett Callaghan. 2014. "Noblesse Oblige? Social Status and Economic Inequality Maintenance Among Politicians." *PLoS ONE* 9 (1): e85293. https://doi.org/10.1371/journal.pone.0085293.

Krumer-Nevo, Michal. 2020. *Radical Hope: Poverty-Aware Practice for Social Work.* Bristol, UK: Policy Press.

Kuca, Grzegorz. 2019. "Electoral Districts." In *Max Planck Encyclopedia of Comparative Constitutional Law.* Oxford: Oxford University Press. https:// doi.org/10.1093/law-mpeccol/e682.013.682.

Kumlin, Staffan, and Bo Rothstein. 2005. "Making and Breaking Social Capital: The Impact of Welfare-State Institutions." *Comparative Political Studies* 38 (4): 339–65. https://doi.org/10.1177/0010414004273203.

Lax, Jeffrey R., Justin H. Phillips, and Alissa F. Stollwerk. 2016. "Are Survey Respondents Lying About Their Support for Same-Sex Marriage? Lessons from a List Experiment." *Public Opinion Quarterly* 80 (2): 510–33. https:// doi.org/10.1093/poq/nfv056.

REFERENCES

Leadership Conference Education Fund. 2019. "Democracy Diverted: Polling Place Closures and the Right to Vote." https://civilrights.org/democracy-diverted/.

Lee, Frances E., and Nolan McCarty. 2019. "The Anxieties of American Democracy." In *Can America Govern Itself?*, ed. Frances E. Lee and Nolan McCarty. Cambridge: Cambridge University Press. https://doi.org/10.1017/9781108667357.001.

Leotti, Sandra M. 2020. "The Discursive Construction of Risk: Social Work Knowledge Production and Criminalized Women." *Social Service Review* 94 (3): 445–87. https://doi.org/10.1086/710562.

Lerner, Josh. 2014. *Everyone Counts: Could "Participatory Budgeting" Change Democracy?* Ithaca, NY: Cornell University Press.

Lewis, John. 2018. "Do Not Get Lost in a Sea of Despair." Twitter. June 27, 2018. https://twitter.com/repjohnlewis/status/1011991303599607808.

Licari, Peter R. 2020. "Sharp as a Fox: Are Foxnews.Com Visitors Less Politically Knowledgeable?" *American Politics Research*, 48 (6): 792–806. https://doi.org/10.1177/1532673X20915222.

Lichter, S. Robert. 2017. "Theories of Media Bias." In *The Oxford Handbook of Political Communication*. Oxford: Oxford University Press.

Lindblom, Charles. 1982. "The Market as Prison." *Journal of Politics* 44 (2): 324–36. https://doi.org/10.2307/2130588.

——. 1995. *Politics and Markets: The World's Political-Economic Systems*. New York: Basic Books.

Link, B. G., E. Susser, A. Stueve, J. Phelan, R. E. Moore, and E. Struening. 1994. "Lifetime and Five-Year Prevalence of Homelessness in the United States." *American Journal of Public Health* 84 (12): 1907–12. https://doi.org/10.2105/AJPH.84.12.1907.

Linn, Suzanna, Jonathan Nagler, and Marco A. Morales. 2010. "Economics, Elections, and Voting Behavior." In *The Oxford Handbook of American Elections and Political Behavior*, ed. Jan E. Leighley. Oxford: Oxford University Press. https://doi.org/10.1093/oxfordhb/9780199235476.003.0020.

Lipsky, Michael. 1984. "Bureaucratic Disentitlement in Social Welfare Programs." *Social Service Review* 58 (1): 3–27.

——. 2010. *Street-Level Bureaucracy: Dilemmas of the Individual in Public Services*. Thirtieth anniversary expanded ed. New York: Russell Sage Foundation.

Losier, Toussaint, and William J. Barber. 2019. "Every Crucifixion Needs a Witness." *Boston Review*, May 28, 2019. https://bostonreview.net/race-politics/toussaint-losier-william-j-barber-ii-every-crucifixion-needs-witness.

Luders, Joseph E. 2010. *The Civil Rights Movement and the Logic of Social Change*. Cambridge: Cambridge University Press.

Lührmann, Anna, Juraj Medzihorsky, Garry Hindle, and Staffan I. Lindberg. 2020. "New Global Data on Political Parties: V-Party." V-Dem Institute briefing paper #9. https://www.v-dem.net/media/filer_public/b6/55/b6553f85 -5c5d-45ec-be63-a48a2abe3f62/briefing_paper_9.pdf?fbclid=IwAR2 J2w72qfyp1Xfu4oaNB2UgYVTAkboM7oQFkfBBn__ptxt_oCrQbahijh4.

Mann, Thomas E., and Norman J. Ornstein. 2016. *It's Even Worse Than It Looks: How the American Constitutional System Collided with the New Politics of Extremism*. New and expanded ed. New York: Basic Books.

Marchese, David. 2020. "Ilhan Omar Is Not Here to Put You at Ease." *New York Times Magazine*, September 21, 2020. https://www.nytimes.com/interactive /2020/09/21/magazine/ilhan-omar-interview.html.

Martin, Courtney E. 2019. "Baby Steps Toward Guaranteed Incomes and Racial Justice." *New York Times*, May 8, 2019. https://www.nytimes.com/2019/05 /08/opinion/baby-steps-toward-guaranteed-incomes-and-racial-justice .html.

Marx, Karl. 1867. "Economic Manuscripts: Capital Vol. I—Chapter Twenty-Five." 1867. https://www.marxists.org/archive/marx/works/1867-c1/ch25.htm.

Masket, Seth. 2020. "Why Political Science Doesn't Like Term Limits." *Mischiefs of Faction*, January 20, 2020. https://www.mischiefsoffaction.com/post /political-science-term-limits.

Matthews, Dylan. 2013. "Graph of the Day: Congress Is Less Popular Than Lice, Colonoscopies and Nickelback." *Washington Post*, January 10, 2013. https:// www.washingtonpost.com/news/wonk/wp/2013/01/10/graph-of-the-day -congress-is-less-popular-than-lice-colonoscopies-and-nickelback/.

Matthews, Morgan C. 2019. "Developments in Gender and U.S. Politics: A Call for Intersectionality." *Sociology Compass* 13 (7): e12716. https://doi.org /10.1111/soc4.12716.

Mattocks, Nicole Olivia. 2018. "Social Action Among Social Work Practitioners: Examining the Micro–Macro Divide." *Social Work* 63 (1): 7–16. https://doi.org/10.1093/sw/swx057.

Mazumder, Soumyajit. 2018. "The Persistent Effect of U.S. Civil Rights Protests on Political Attitudes." *American Journal of Political Science* 62 (4): 922–35. https://doi.org/10.1111/ajps.12384.

McAdam, Doug. 1999. *Political Process and the Development of Black Insurgency, 1930–1970*. 2nd ed. Chicago: University of Chicago Press.

McAuliffe, Colin. 2019. "The Senate Is an Irredeemable Institution." Data for Progress. https://www.dataforprogress.org/memos/the-senate-is-an-irredeemable-institution.

McCarty, Nolan M. 2019. *Polarization: What Everyone Needs to Know*. New York: Oxford University Press.

McDonald, Michael. 2020. "National General Election VEP Turnout Rates, 1789–Present." United States Election Project. http://www.electproject.org/national-1789-present.

McIntosh, Kriston, Emily Moss, Ryan Nunn, and Jay Shambaugh. 2020. "Examining the Black-White Wealth Gap." *Brookings* (blog). February 27, 2020. https://www.brookings.edu/blog/up-front/2020/02/27/examining-the-black-white-wealth-gap/.

McKay, Amy Melissa. 2018. "Fundraising for Favors? Linking Lobbyist-Hosted Fundraisers to Legislative Benefits." *Political Research Quarterly* 71 (4): 869–80. https://doi.org/10.1177/1065912918771745.

Mettler, Suzanne. 2002. "Bringing the State Back In to Civic Engagement: Policy Feedback Effects of the G.I. Bill for World War II Veterans." *American Political Science Review* 96 (2): 351–65. https://doi.org/10.1017/S0003055402000217.

——. 2005a. *Soldiers to Citizens: The G.I. Bill and the Making of the Greatest Generation*. New York: Oxford University Press.

——. 2005b. " 'The Only Good Thing Was the G.I. Bill': Effects of the Education and Training Provisions on African-American Veterans' Political Participation." *Studies in American Political Development* 19 (1): 31–52. https://doi.org/10.1017/S0898588X05000027.

——. 2011. *The Submerged State: How Invisible Government Policies Undermine American Democracy*. Chicago: University of Chicago Press.

——. 2019. "Making What Government Does Apparent to Citizens: Policy Feedback Effects, Their Limitations, and How They Might Be Facilitated." *The ANNALS of the American Academy of Political and Social Science* 685 (1): 30–46. https://doi.org/10.1177/0002716219860108.

Mettler, Suzanne, and Robert C. Lieberman. 2020. *Four Threats: The Recurring Crises of American Democracy*. New York: St. Martin's.

Mettler, Suzanne, and Andrew Milstein. 2007. "American Political Development from Citizens' Perspective: Tracking Federal Government's Presence in Individual Lives Over Time." *Studies in American Political Development* 21 (1): 110–30. https://doi.org/10.1017/S0898588X07000156.

Mettler, Suzanne, and Jeffrey M. Stonecash. 2008. "Government Program Usage and Political Voice." *Social Science Quarterly* 89 (2): 273–93. https://doi.org/10.1111/j.1540-6237.2008.00532.x.

Michener, Jamila. 2018. *Fragmented Democracy: Medicaid, Federalism, and Unequal Politics*. New York: Cambridge University Press.

Miller, Joanne M., Kyle L. Saunders, and Christina E. Farhart. 2016. "Conspiracy Endorsement as Motivated Reasoning: The Moderating Roles of Political Knowledge and Trust." *American Journal of Political Science* 60 (4): 824–44. https://doi.org/10.1111/ajps.12234.

Millhiser, Ian. 2020. "The Danger the Supreme Court Poses to Democracy, in Just Two Numbers." Vox. October 26, 2020. https://www.vox.com/2020/10/26/21534358/supreme-court-amy-coney-barrett-constitution-anti-democratic-electoral-college-senate.

Mills, C. Wright. 2000. *The Power Elite*. New York: Oxford University Press.

Minieri, Joan, and Paul Getsos. 2007. *Tools for Radical Democracy: How to Organize for Power in Your Community*. San Francisco: Jossey-Bass.

Minnite, Lorraine Carol. 2010. *The Myth of Voter Fraud*. Ithaca, NY: Cornell University Press.

Misra, Jordan. 2019. "Voter Turnout Rates Among All Voting Age and Major Racial and Ethnic Groups Were Higher Than in 2014." U.S. Census Bureau. https://www.census.gov/library/stories/2019/04/behind-2018-united-states-midterm-election-turnout.html.

Mitchell, Amy, Mark Jurkowitz, J. Baxter Oliphant, and Elisa Shearer. 2020. "Americans Who Mainly Get Their News on Social Media Are Less Engaged, Less Knowledgeable." *Pew Research Center's Journalism Project* (blog). July 30, 2020. https://www.journalism.org/2020/07/30/americans-who-mainly-get-their-news-on-social-media-are-less-engaged-less-knowledgeable/.

Moch, Marilynn. 2009. "A Critical Understanding of Social Work by Paolo Freire: Social Workers World Conference, Stockholm, Sweden, July 30, 1988." *Journal of Progressive Human Services* 20 (1): 92–97. https://doi.org/10.1080/10428230902878285.

Mohanty, Abinash. 2019. "Poverty Dynamics: An Overview of Longitudinal Poverty Estimates Produced by the United States Census Bureau." U.S. Census Bureau. https://unece.org/fileadmin/DAM/stats/documents/ece/ces/ge.15/2019/mtg2/PPP_6_Longitudinal_US_Census_Bureau.pdf.

Morin, Rich, Paul Taylor, and Eileen Patten. 2012. "A Bipartisan Nation of Beneficiaries." Pew Research Center. https://www.pewresearch.org/social-trends/2012/12/18/a-bipartisan-nation-of-beneficiaries/.

REFERENCES

Moynihan, Donald P., and Joe Soss. 2014. "Policy Feedback and the Politics of Administration." *Public Administration Review* 74 (3): 320–32. https://doi.org/10.1111/puar.12200.

Mullainathan, Sendhil, and Eldar Shafir. 2013. *Scarcity: Why Having Too Little Means So Much.* New York: Times Books.

Mutz, Diana C. 2018. "Status Threat, Not Economic Hardship, Explains the 2016 Presidential Vote." *Proceedings of the National Academy of Sciences* 115 (19): E4330–39. https://doi.org/10.1073/pnas.1718155115.

Nagel, Thomas. 1989. *The View from Nowhere.* New York: Oxford University Press.

National Association of Social Workers. 2017. "NASW Code of Ethics." https://www.socialworkers.org/About/Ethics/Code-of-Ethics/Code-of-Ethics-English.

National Association of Social Workers, Kathryn Conley Wehrmann, and Angelo McClain. 2018. *Social Work Speaks: National Association of Social Workers Policy Statements, 2018–2020.* Washington, DC: NASW Press.

Neustadt, Richard E. 1991. *Presidential Power and the Modern Presidents: The Politics of Leadership from Roosevelt to Reagan.* New York: Free Press.

Newkirk, Vann R., II. 2017. "How Redistricting Became a Technological Arms Race." *Atlantic,* October 28, 2017. https://www.theatlantic.com/politics/archive/2017/10/gerrymandering-technology-redmap-2020/543888/.

Newport, Frank. 2017. "Americans Favor Compromise to Get Things Done in Washington." Gallup. https://news.gallup.com/poll/220265/americans-favor-compromise-things-done-washington.aspx.

———. 2019. "Social Security and American Public Opinion." Gallup. https://news.gallup.com/opinion/polling-matters/258335/social-security-american-public-opinion.aspx.

Nyhan, Brendan. 2009. "The Green Lantern Theory of the Presidency." *Brendan Nyhan* (blog). December 14, 2009. https://www.brendan-nyhan.com/blog/2009/12/the-green-lantern-theory-of-the-presidency.html.

Oberlander, Jonathan. 2007. "Learning from Failure in Health Care Reform." *New England Journal of Medicine* 357 (17): 1677–79. https://doi.org/10.1056/NEJMp078201.

O'Connor, Julia S., Ann Shola Orloff, and Sheila Shaver. 1999. *States, Markets, Families: Gender, Liberalism, and Social Policy in Australia, Canada, Great Britain, and the United States.* Cambridge: Cambridge University Press.

OECD. 2018. *A Broken Social Elevator? How to Promote Social Mobility.* https://doi.org/10.1787/9789264301085-en.

———. 2020a. "OECD Data." http://data.oecd.org.

——. 2020b. "OECD Economic Surveys: United States 2020." https://www
.oecd-ilibrary.org/sites/10ddc549-en/index.html?itemId=/content/component
/10ddc549-en.

——. 2020c. "Social Spending." *OECD Data* (blog). https://data.oecd.org
/socialexp/social-spending.htm.

Olson, Mancur. 2003. *The Logic of Collective Action: Public Goods and the Theory
of Groups.* Cambridge, MA: Harvard University Press.

OpenSecrets.org. 2020. "Interest Groups." https://www.opensecrets.org
/industries/.

Organizational Research Services. 2004. "Theory of Change: A Practical Tool."
https://www.aecf.org/resources/theory-of-change/.

Ostrander, Jason A., Janelle Bryan, and Shannon R. Lane. 2019. "Clinical Social
Workers, Gender, and Perceptions of Political Participation." *Advances in
Social Work* 19 (1): 256–75. https://doi.org/10.18060/22609.

Page, Benjamin I., and Martin Gilens. 2017. *Democracy in America? What Has Gone
Wrong and What We Can Do About It.* Chicago: University of Chicago Press.

Page, Benjamin I., and Lawrence R. Jacobs. 2009. *Class War? What Americans
Really Think About Economic Inequality.* Chicago: University of Chicago Press.

Page, Benjamin I., and Robert Y. Shapiro. 1982. "Changes in Americans' Policy
Preferences, 1935–1979." *Public Opinion Quarterly* 46 (1): 24–42.

Parker, Trey. 1998. "Gnomes." *South Park.* Season 2, episode 17. Comedy Central.

Parolin, Zachary, Megan A. Curran, and Christopher Wimer. 2020. "The
CARES Act and Poverty in the COVID-19 Crisis." Columbia University:
Center on Poverty and Social Policy. https://www.povertycenter.columbia
.edu/news-internal/coronavirus-cares-act-forecasting-poverty-estimates.

Peck, Sarah Herman. 2018. "Congress's Power Over Courts: Jurisdiction Strip-
ping and the Rule of Klein." Congressional Research Service. https://fas
.org/sgp/crs/misc/R44967.pdf.

Perliger, Arie. 2012. "Challengers from the Sidelines: Understanding America's
Violent Far-Right." Combating Terrorism Center at West Point.

Persily, Nathaniel, and Jon Cohen. 2016. "Americans Are Losing Faith in
Democracy—and in Each Other." *Washington Post*, October 14, 2016.
https://www.washingtonpost.com/opinions/americans-are-losing-faith
-in-democracy—and-in-each-other/2016/10/14/b35234ea-90c6-11e6-9c52
-0b10449e33c4_story.html.

Pew Research Center. 2018a. "Political Engagement, Knowledge and the
Midterms." https://www.pewresearch.org/politics/2018/04/26/10-political
-engagement-knowledge-and-the-midterms/.

———. 2018b. "An Examination of the 2016 Electorate, Based on Validated Voters." *Pew Research Center—U.S. Politics & Policy* (blog). August 9, 2018. https://www.pewresearch.org/politics/2018/08/09/an-examination-of-the-2016-electorate-based-on-validated-voters/.

———. 2019a. "Political Independents: Who They Are, What They Think." *Pew Research Center—U.S. Politics & Policy* (blog). March 14, 2019. https://www.pewresearch.org/politics/2019/03/14/political-independents-who-they-are-what-they-think/.

———. 2019b. "Public Trust in Government: 1958–2019." https://www.pewresearch.org/politics/2019/04/11/public-trust-in-government-1958-2019/.

———. 2019c. "Changing Attitudes on Same-Sex Marriage." *Pew Research Center's Religion & Public Life Project* (blog). May 14, 2019. https://www.pewforum.org/fact-sheet/changing-attitudes-on-gay-marriage/.

———. 2019d. "Public Opinion on Abortion." *Pew Research Center's Religion & Public Life Project* (blog). August 29, 2019. https://www.pewforum.org/fact-sheet/public-opinion-on-abortion/.

Phillips, Scott, and Justin F. Marceau. 2020. "Whom the State Kills." SSRN Scholarly Paper ID 3440828. Rochester, NY: Social Science Research Network. https://doi.org/10.2139/ssrn.3440828.

Pierson, Paul, and Eric Schickler. 2020. "Madison's Constitution Under Stress: A Developmental Analysis of Political Polarization." *Annual Review of Political Science* 23 (1): 37–58. https://doi.org/10.1146/annurev-polisci-050718-033629.

Piketty, Thomas. 2017. *Capital in the Twenty-First Century*, trans. Arthur Goldhammer. Cambridge, MA: Harvard University Press. https://www.overdrive.com/search?q=2B4A656F-5110-495D-894E-0CC5348B4C48.

Pimpare, Stephen. 2004. *The New Victorians: Poverty, Politics, and Propaganda in Two Gilded Ages*. New York: New Press.

———. 2007. "An African American Welfare State." *New Political Science* 29 (3): 313–31. https://doi.org/10.1080/07393140701523643.

———. 2008. *A People's History of Poverty in America*. New York: New Press.

Piven, Frances Fox. 2006. *Challenging Authority: How Ordinary People Change America*. Lanham, MD: Rowman.

———. 2017. "Throw Sand in the Gears of Everything." *Nation*, January 18, 2017. https://www.thenation.com/article/archive/throw-sand-in-the-gears-of-everything/.

Piven, Frances Fox, and Richard A. Cloward. 1966. "The Weight of the Poor: A Strategy to End Poverty." *Nation*, May 2, 1966. https://www.thenation.com/article/archive/weight-poor-strategy-end-poverty/.

——. 1979. *Poor People's Movements: Why They Succeed, How They Fail*. New York: Vintage.

——. 1993. *Regulating the Poor: The Functions of Public Welfare*. Updated ed. New York: Vintage.

——. 2000. *Why Americans Still Don't Vote: And Why Politicians Want It That Way*. Rev. and updated ed. Boston: Beacon.

Polsky, Andrew Joseph. 1993. *The Rise of the Therapeutic State*. Princeton, NJ: Princeton University Press.

Poppendieck, Janet. 1999. *Sweet Charity?: Emergency Food and the End of Entitlement*. New York: Penguin.

Popple, Philip R. and Leslie Leighninger. 2001. *The Policy-Based Profession: An Introduction to Social Welfare Policy Analysis for Social Workers*. Boston: Allyn and Bacon.

Portland State University and the Knight Foundation. 2016. "Who Votes for Mayor?" 2016. http://www.whovotesformayor.org/.

Powell, Lynda W. 2014. "The Influence of Campaign Contributions on the Legislative Process." *Duke Journal of Constitutional Law & Public Policy* 9 (1): 75–101.

Prison Policy Initiative. 2020. "Prison Populations and the Census." August 10, 2020. https://www.prisonersofthecensus.org/faq.html.

Pritzker, Suzanne, and Shannon R. Lane. 2017. "Political Social Work: History, Forms, and Opportunities for Innovation." *Social Work* 62 (1): 80–82. https://doi.org/10.1093/sw/sww072.

Prosser, Christopher, and Jonathan Mellon. 2018. "The Twilight of the Polls? A Review of Trends in Polling Accuracy and the Causes of Polling Misses." *Government and Opposition* 53 (4): 757–90. https://doi.org/10.1017/gov.2018.7.

Public Policy Polling. 2013. "Congress Less Popular Than Cockroaches, Traffic Jams." https://www.publicpolicypolling.com/wp-content/uploads/2017/09/PPP_Release_Natl_010813_.pdf.

Putnam, Lara, Erica Chenoweth, and Jeremy Pressman. 2020. "The Floyd Protests Are the Broadest in U.S. History—and Are Spreading to White, Small-Town America." *Washington Post*, June 6, 2020. https://www.washingtonpost.com/politics/2020/06/06/floyd-protests-are-broadest-us-history-are-spreading-white-small-town-america/.

Rakich, Nathaniel. 2021. "Why So Few Absentee Ballots Were Rejected in 2020." *FiveThirtyEight* (blog). February 17, 2021. https://fivethirtyeight.com/features/why-so-few-absentee-ballots-were-rejected-in-2020/.

Rank, Mark R. 2007. "Rethinking the Scope and Impact of Poverty in the United States." *Connecticut Public Interest Law Journal* 6 (2): 165–81.

———. 2009. "Measuring the Economic Racial Divide Across the Course of American Lives." *Race and Social Problems* 1 (2): 57–66. https://doi.org/10.1007/s12552-009-9009-z.

Rank, Mark R., and Thomas A. Hirschl. 2002. "Welfare Use as a Life Course Event: Toward a New Understanding of the U.S. Social Safety Net." *Social Work* 47 (3): 237–48. https://doi.org/10.1093/sw/47.3.237.

———. 2009. "Estimating the Risk of Food Stamp Use and Impoverishment During Childhood." *Archives of Pediatrics & Adolescent Medicine* 163 (11): 994–99. https://doi.org/10.1001/archpediatrics.2009.178.

———. 2015. "The Likelihood of Experiencing Relative Poverty Over the Life Course." *PLoS ONE* 10 (7): e0133513. https://doi.org/10.1371/journal.pone.0133513.

———. 2020. "Poverty Risk Calculator." *Confronting Poverty* (blog). 2020. https://confrontingpoverty.org/poverty-risk-calculator/.

Rank, Mark R., Thomas A. Hirschl, and Kirk A. Foster. 2016. *Chasing the American Dream: Understanding What Shapes Our Fortunes.* New York: Oxford University Press.

Rasmussen, Cameron, and Kirk "Jae" James. 2020. "Trading Cops for Social Workers Isn't the Solution to Police Violence." *Truthout*, July 17, 2020. https://truthout.org/articles/trading-cops-for-social-workers-isnt-the-solution-to-police-violence/.

Rauchway, Eric. 2008. *The Great Depression & the New Deal: A Very Short Introduction.* New York: Oxford University Press.

———. 2018. *Winter War: Hoover, Roosevelt, and the First Clash Over the New Deal.* New York: Basic Books.

Reardon, Sean F., and Ann Owens. 2014. "60 Years After *Brown*: Trends and Consequences of School Segregation." *Annual Review of Sociology* 40 (1): 199–218. https://doi.org/10.1146/annurev-soc-071913-043152.

Reingold, Beth, Kerry Lee Haynie, and Kirsten Widner. 2021. *Race, Gender, and Political Representation: Toward a More Intersectional Approach.* New York: Oxford University Press.

Reisch, Michael, and Janice Andrews. 2002. *The Road Not Taken: A History of Radical Social Work in the United States.* 4th ed. New York: Brunner-Routledge.

Remler, Dahlia K., and Sherry A. Glied. 2003. "What Other Programs Can Teach Us: Increasing Participation in Health Insurance Programs." *American Journal of Public Health* 93 (1): 67–74.

Reynolds, Molly E. 2020. "What Is the Senate Filibuster, and What Would It Take to Eliminate It?" *Brookings* (blog). September 9, 2020. https://www.brookings.edu/policy2020/votervital/what-is-the-senate-filibuster-and-what-would-it-take-to-eliminate-it/.

Richan, Willard C. 2006. *Lobbying for Social Change.* 3rd ed. New York: Haworth.

Roberts, David. 2018. "The Real Problem with the New York Times Op-Ed Page: It's Not Honest About US Conservatism." Vox. March 15, 2018. https://www.vox.com/policy-and-politics/2018/3/15/17113176/new-york-times-opinion-page-conservatism.

Roberts, John. 2005. *Confirmation Hearing on the Nomination of John G. Roberts, Jr. to Be Chief Justice of the United States.* https://www.judiciary.senate.gov/imo/media/doc/GPO-CHRG-ROBERTS.pdf.

Robin, Corey. 2018. *The Reactionary Mind: Conservatism from Edmund Burke to Donald Trump.* 2nd ed. New York: Oxford University Press.

Rocha, Cynthia J. 2007. *Essentials of Social Work Policy Practice.* Hoboken, NJ: Wiley.

Rosen, Jay. 2010. "The View from Nowhere: Questions and Answers." Press-Think. November 10, 2010. https://pressthink.org/2010/11/the-view-from-nowhere-questions-and-answers/.

Rosenbaum, Dottie, and Brynne Keith-Jennings. 2019. "SNAP Caseload and Spending Declines Have Accelerated in Recent Years." Center on Budget and Policy Priorities. https://www.cbpp.org/research/food-assistance/snap-caseload-and-spending-declines-have-accelerated-in-recent-years#_ftn3.

Rothman, J., and T. Mizrahi. 2014. "Balancing Micro and Macro Practice: A Challenge for Social Work." *Social Work* 59 (1): 91–93. https://doi.org/10.1093/sw/swt067.

Rowntree, B. Seebohm. 1901. *Poverty, a Study of Town Life.* London: Macmillan.

Rubin, Allen. 2012. "Civilian Social Work with Veterans Returning from Iraq and Afghanistan: A Call to Action." *Social Work* 57 (4): 293–96. https://doi.org/10.1093/sw/sws048.

Russell, Annelise. 2018. "U.S. Senators on Twitter: Asymmetric Party Rhetoric in 140 Characters." *American Politics Research* 46 (4): 695–723. https://doi.org/10.1177/1532673X17715619.

Rutenberg, Jim, and Nick Corasaniti. 2020. "Behind Trump's Yearslong Effort to Turn Losing Into Winning." *New York Times,* November 15, 2020. https://www.nytimes.com/2020/11/15/us/politics/trump-voter-fraud-claims.html.

Saez, Emmanuel, and Gabriel Zucman. 2016. "Wealth Inequality in the United States Since 1913: Evidence from Capitalized Income Tax Data." *Quarterly Journal of Economics* 131 (2): 519–78. https://doi.org/10.1093/qje/qjw004.

——. 2019. *The Triumph of Injustice: How the Rich Dodge Taxes and How to Make Them Pay.* New York: Norton.

——. 2020. "The Rise of Income and Wealth Inequality in America: Evidence from Distributional Macroeconomic Accounts." *Journal of Economic Perspectives* 34 (4): 3–26. https://doi.org/10.1257/jep.34.4.3.

Saloner, Brendan, Kalind Parish, Julie A. Ward, Grace DiLaura, and Sharon Dolovich. 2020. "COVID-19 Cases and Deaths in Federal and State Prisons." *JAMA* 324 (6): 602–3. https://doi.org/10.1001/jama.2020.12528.

Sawhill, Isabel V., and Christopher Pulliam. 2019. "Americans Want the Wealthy and Corporations to Pay More Taxes, but Are Elected Officials Listening?" *Brookings* (blog). March 14, 2019. https://www.brookings.edu/blog/up-front/2019/03/14/americans-want-the-wealthy-and-corporations-to-pay-more-taxes-but-are-elected-officials-listening/.

Schakel, Wouter, Brian Burgoon, and Armen Hakhverdian. 2020. "Real but Unequal Representation in Welfare State Reform." *Politics & Society* 48 (1): 131–63. https://doi.org/10.1177/0032329219897984.

Schattschneider, E. E. (1960) 1975. *The Semisovereign People: A Realist's View of Democracy in America.* Hinsdale, IL: Dryden.

Schein, Aaron, Keyon Vafa, Dhanya Sridhar, Victor Veitch, Jeffrey Quinn, James Moffet, David M. Blei, and Donald P. Green. 2020. "A Digital Field Experiment Reveals Large Effects of Friend-to-Friend Texting on Voter Turnout." SSRN. https://papers.ssrn.com/sol3/papers.cfm?abstract_id=3696179.

Schlozman, Kay Lehman, Henry A. Brady, and Sidney Verba. 2020. *Unequal and Unrepresented: Political Inequality and the People's Voice in the New Gilded Age.* Princeton, NJ: Princeton University Press.

Schmitt, John, Elise Gould, and Josh Bivens. 2018. "America's Slow-Motion Wage Crisis: Four Decades of Slow and Unequal Growth." Economic Policy Institute. https://www.epi.org/publication/americas-slow-motion-wage-crisis-four-decades-of-slow-and-unequal-growth-2/.

Schneider, Anne, and Helen Ingram. 1993. "Social Construction of Target Populations: Implications for Politics and Policy." *American Political Science Review* 87 (2): 334–47. https://doi.org/10.2307/2939044.

Schram, Sanford. 2002. *Praxis for the Poor: Piven and Cloward and the Future of Social Science in Social Welfare.* New York: New York University Press.

Scott, James C. 2000. *Weapons of the Weak: Everyday Forms of Peasant Resistance.* New Haven, CT: Yale University Press.

Semega, Jessica, Melissa Kollar, Emily A. Shrider, and John Creamer. 2020. "Income and Poverty in the United States: 2019." U.S. Census Bureau. https://www.census.gov/library/publications/2020/demo/p60-270.html.

Shafer, Kevin, and Douglas Wendt. 2015. "Men's Mental Health: A Call to Social Workers." *Social Work* 60 (2): 105–12. https://doi.org/10.1093/sw/swu061.

Shdaimah, Corey S., Roland W. Stahl, and Sanford Schram. 2011. *Change Research: A Case Study on Collaborative Methods for Social Workers and Advocates.* New York: Columbia University Press.

Sheingate, Adam. 2014. "Institutional Dynamics and American Political Development." *Annual Review of Political Science* 17 (1): 461–77. https://doi.org/10.1146/annurev-polisci-040113-161139.

Shubber, Kadhim. 2020. "Lawsuit Tracker: Trump's Battle Faces Tough Test This Week." November 16, 2020. https://www.ft.com/content/20b114b5-5419-493b-9923-a918a2527931.

Sides, John, and Lynn Vavreck. 2013. *The Gamble: Choice and Chance in the 2012 Presidential Election.* Princeton, NJ: Princeton University Press.

Sides, John, Lynn Vavreck, and Christopher Warshaw. 2020. "The Effect of Television Advertising in United States Elections." http://chriswarshaw.com/papers/advertising.pdf.

Simon, Herbert A. 1997. *Administrative Behavior: A Study of Decision-Making Processes in Administrative Organizations.* 4th ed. New York: Free Press.

Skowronek, Stephen. 1997. *The Politics Presidents Make: Leadership from John Adams to Bill Clinton.* Cambridge, MA: Belknap Press.

Smith, Rogers M. 1993. "Beyond Tocqueville, Myrdal, and Hartz: The Multiple Traditions in America." *American Political Science Review* 87 (3): 549–66. https://doi.org/10.2307/2938735.

———. 2015. "Political Science and the Public Sphere Today." *Perspectives on Politics* 13 (2): 366–76. https://doi.org/10.1017/S1537592715000225.

Soboroff, Jacob. 2020. *Separated: Inside an American Tragedy.* New York: William Morrow.

Social Security Administration. n.d. "Social Security History." https://www.ssa.gov/history/law.html.

Soss, Joe. 1999. "Lessons of Welfare: Policy Design, Political Learning, and Political Action." *American Political Science Review* 93 (2): 363–80. https://doi.org/10.2307/2585401.

Soss, Joe, and Lawrence R. Jacobs. 2009. "The Place of Inequality: Non-Participation in the American Polity." *Political Science Quarterly* 124 (1): 95–125. https://doi.org/10.1002/j.1538-165X.2009.tb00643.x.

Sotomayor, Frank O. 2020. "Reporting on Polls? Here's How to Do It Responsibly." *Poynter* (blog). September 24, 2020. https://www.poynter.org/ethics-trust /2020/reporting-on-polls-heres-how-to-do-it-responsibly/.

Spade, Dean. 2020. *Mutual Aid: Building Solidarity During This Crisis (and the Next)*. London: Verso.

Specht, Harry and Mark E. Courtney. 1995. *Unfaithful Angels: How Social Work Has Abandoned its Mission*. New York: Free Press.

Steinmo, Sven. 1995. "Why Is Government So Small in America?" *Governance* 8 (3): 303–34. https://doi.org/10.1111/j.1468-0491.1995.tb00213.x.

Stepan, Alfred, and Juan J. Linz. 2011. "Comparative Perspectives on Inequality and the Quality of Democracy in the United States." *Perspectives on Politics* 9 (4): 841–56. https://doi.org/10.1017/S1537592711003756.

Stevens, Stuart. 2020. *It Was All a Lie: How the Republican Party Became Donald Trump*. New York: Knopf.

Stevenson, Margaret C., Bette L. Bottoms, and Kelly C. Burke, eds. 2020. *The Legacy of Racism for Children: Psychology, Law, and Public Policy*. New York: Oxford University Press.

Stone, Deborah. 2012. *Policy Paradox: The Art of Political Decision Making*. 3rd ed. New York: Norton.

Sullivan, Margaret. 2020. *Ghosting the News: Local Journalism and the Crisis of American Democracy*. New York: Columbia Global Reports.

Summers, Juana. 2020. "Trump Push to Invalidate Votes in Heavily Black Cities Alarms Civil Rights Groups." NPR. November 24, 2020. https://www .npr.org/2020/11/24/938187233/trump-push-to-invalidate-votes-in-heavily -black-cities-alarms-civil-rights-group.

Taibbi, Matt. 2005. "Inside the Horror Show That Is Congress." *Rolling Stone* (blog). August 25, 2005. https://www.rollingstone.com/feature/inside-the -horror-show-that-is-congress-177955/.

Tate, Julie, Jennifer Jenkins, and Steven Rich. 2020. "Fatal Force: Police Shootings Database." Washington Post. https://www.washingtonpost.com/graphics /investigations/police-shootings-database/.

Tax Policy Center. 2020. "Briefing Book: What Are the Tax Benefits of Home Ownership?" https://www.taxpolicycenter.org/briefing-book/what-are-tax -benefits-homeownership.

Teles, Steven M. 2013. "Kludgeocracy in America." *National Affairs*. https://www.nationalaffairs.com/publications/detail/kludgeocracy-in-america.

Thomsen, Danielle M. 2014. "Ideological Moderates Won't Run: How Party Fit Matters for Partisan Polarization in Congress." *Journal of Politics* 76 (3): 786–97. https://doi.org/10.1017/S0022381614000243.

Thoreau, Henry David. (1849) 2017. *Civil Disobedience and Other Essays*. Digireads.com.

Thurber, James A., and Antoine Yoshinaka. 2015. *American Gridlock: The Sources, Character, and Impact of Political Polarization*. Cambridge: Cambridge University Press.

Tikkanen, Roosa, and Melinda K. Abrams. 2020. "U.S. Health Care from a Global Perspective, 2019: Higher Spending, Worse Outcomes." The Commonwealth Fund. January 30, 2020. https://doi.org/10.26099/7avy-fc29.

Tocqueville, Alexis de. (1835–1840) 2004. *Democracy in America*. New York: Library of America.

Torney-Purta, Judith, and Carolyn Henry Barber. 2004. "Strengths and Weaknesses in U.S. Students' Knowledge and Skills: Analysis from the IEA Civic Education Study." https://circle.tufts.edu/sites/default/files/2019-12/FS_StrengthsWeaknessesinUSStudentsKnowledgeSkills_2007.pdf.

Turberville, Sarah, and Anthony Marcum. 2018. "Those 5-to-4 Decisions on the Supreme Court? 9 to 0 Is Far More Common." *Washington Post*, June 28, 2018. https://www.washingtonpost.com/news/posteverything/wp/2018/06/28/those-5-4-decisions-on-the-supreme-court-9-0-is-far-more-common/.

Uggen, Christopher, Sarah Shannon, and Arleth Pulido-Nava. 2020. "Locked Out 2020: Estimates of People Denied Voting Rights Due to a Felony Conviction." The Sentencing Project. https://www.sentencingproject.org/publications/locked-out-2020-estimates-of-people-denied-voting-rights-due-to-a-felony-conviction/.

U.S. Bureau of Labor Statistics. 2020. "Alternative Measures of Labor Underutilization." 2020. https://www.bls.gov/charts/employment-situation/alternative-measures-of-labor-underutilization.htm.

U.S. Census Bureau. 2017a. "2017 National Population Projections Tables: Main Series." https://www.census.gov/data/tables/2017/demo/popproj/2017-summary-tables.html.

——. 2017b. "Voting and Registration in the Election of November 2016." https://www.census.gov/data/tables/time-series/demo/voting-and-registration/p20-580.html.

——. 2020. "Historical Poverty Tables: People and Families—1959 to 2018." https://www.census.gov/data/tables/time-series/demo/income-poverty /historical-poverty-people.html.

U.S. Department of Homeland Security. 2009. "Rightwing Extremism: Current Economic and Political Climate Fueling Resurgence in Radicalization and Recruitment." Office of Intelligence and Analysis. https://fas.org/irp /eprint/rightwing.pdf

——.2020."HomelandThreatAssessment October 2020."https://www.dhs.gov /sites/default/files/publications/2020_10_06_homeland-threat-assessment .pdf.

U.S. Department of Housing and Urban Development. 2020. "HUD's Proposed 2021 budget." https://www.hud.gov/budget#:~:text=On%20February%20 10%2C%202020%2C%20the,health%20and%20safety%20hazards%3B%20and.

U.S. Election Assistance Commission. 2017. "The Election Administration and Voting Survey: 2016 Comprehensive Report." https://www.wric.com/wp -content/uploads/sites/74/2020/10/2016_EAVS_Comprehensive_Report.pdf.

USDA Economic Research Service. 2020. "Population." May 13, 2020. https:// data.ers.usda.gov/reports.aspx?ID=17827#P6d1697b4c6eb4c2da7b2a485e0d2cf91 _2_138iT3.

USDA Food and Nutrition Service. 2019. "Trends in SNAP Participation Rates: Fiscal Year 2010–2017." https://www.fns.usda.gov/snap/trends-supplemental -nutrition-assistance-program-participation-rates-fiscal-year-2010.

Vandermaas-Peeler, Alex, Daniel Cox, Molly Fisch-Friedman, Rob Griffin, and Robert P. Jones. 2018. "American Democracy in Crisis: The Challenges of Voter Knowledge, Participation, and Polarization." Public Religion Research Institute. https://www.prri.org/research/american-democracy-in-crisis-voters -midterms-trump-election-2018/.

VanderMolen, Kathryn. 2017. "Stealth Democracy Revisited: Reconsidering Preferences for Less Visible Government." *Political Research Quarterly* 70 (3): 687–98. https://doi.org/10.1177/1065912917712478.

Villarreal Sosa, Leticia, and Raylinn Nuckolls. 2018. "School Social Workers: A Call to Action in Support of Human Rights." *International Journal of School Social Work* 3 (1). https://doi.org/10.4148/2161-4148.1038.

Wagner, David. 2000. *What's Love Got to Do with It?: A Critical Look at American Charity.* New York: New Press.

Wagner, Peter, and Wendy Sawyer. 2018. "States of Incarceration: The Global Context 2018." Prison Policy Project. https://www.prisonpolicy.org/global /2018.html.

REFERENCES

Wallach, Philip A. 2015. "Government Decoherence and Its Discontents." *Law & Liberty* (blog). September 1, 2015. https://lawliberty.org/forum/government-decoherence-and-its-discontents/.

Weaver, Vesla M., and Amy E. Lerman. 2010. "Political Consequences of the Carceral State." *American Political Science Review* 104 (4): 817–33. https://doi.org/10.1017/S0003055410000456.

Weaver, Vesla, Gwen Prowse, and Spencer Piston. 2019. "Too Much Knowledge, Too Little Power: An Assessment of Political Knowledge in Highly Policed Communities." *Journal of Politics* 81 (3): 1153–66. https://doi.org/10.1086/703538.

Weber, Max. (1919) 1965. *Politics as a Vocation*. Philadelphia: Fortress.

Wegman, Jesse. 2020. *Let the People Pick the President: The Case for Abolishing the Electoral College*. New York: St. Martin's.

Weill, Matthew, Charles Stewart, Tim Harper, and Christopher Thomas. 2019. "The 2018 Voting Experience: Polling Place Lines." Bipartisan Policy Center. https://bipartisanpolicy.org/report/the-2018-voting-experience/.

Wenocur, Stanley, and Michael Reisch. 1989. *From Charity to Enterprise: The Development of American Social Work in a Market Economy*. Urbana: University of Illinois Press.

WHCA. 2006. *2006 White House Correspondents' Dinner*. C-SPAN. https://www.c-span.org/video/?192243-1/2006-white-house-correspondents-dinner.

Williams, Mark T. 2019. "MLB Umpires Missed 34,294 Pitch Calls in 2018. Time for Robo-Umps?" *BU Today*. Boston University. https://www.bu.edu/articles/2019/mlb-umpires-strike-zone-accuracy/.

Williamson, Vanessa. 2019. "Public Ignorance or Elitist Jargon? Reconsidering Americans' Overestimates of Government Waste and Foreign Aid." *American Politics Research* 47 (1): 152–73. https://doi.org/10.1177/1532673X18759645.

Woodly, Deva. 2018. "The Importance of Public Meaning for Political Persuasion." *Perspectives on Politics* 16 (1): 22–35. https://doi.org/10.1017/S1537592717003127.

Woolhandler, Steffie, and David U. Himmelstein. 2019. "Single-Payer Reform—'Medicare for All.'" *JAMA* 321 (24): 2399–2400. https://doi.org/10.1001/jama.2019.7031.

World Bank. 2019. "Proportion of Seats Held by Women in National Parliaments (%) | Data." 2019. https://data.worldbank.org/indicator/SG.GEN.PARL.ZS?most_recent_value_desc=false.

——. 2020. "Mortality Rate, Infant (per 1,000 Live Births) | Data." 2020. https://data.worldbank.org/indicator/SP.DYN.IMRT.IN?most_recent_value_desc=false.

Wouters, Olivier J. 2020. "Lobbying Expenditures and Campaign Contributions by the Pharmaceutical and Health Product Industry in the United States, 1999–2018." *JAMA Internal Medicine* 180 (5): 688–97. https://doi.org/10.1001/jamainternmed.2020.0146.

Yglesias, Matthew. 2018. "The Case for Fox News Studies." *Political Communication* 35 (4): 681–83. https://doi.org/10.1080/10584609.2018.1477532.

Zaller, John. 1992. *The Nature and Origins of Mass Opinion*. Cambridge: Cambridge University Press.

INDEX